Eight to Great

Eight Steps to Delivering an Exceptional Customer Experience

by GREG GIANFORTE

Eight to Great

*Eight Steps to Delivering an Exceptional
Customer Experience*

Table of Contents

From the Author

This book is intended for anyone tasked with, interested in, or responsible for attracting and retaining customers. My decision to write the book grew out of more than twenty years of experience starting and building companies. Along the way, I've learned a great deal about taking care of customers—and I've included that advice here. I've found that satisfied customers can be your strongest advocates, and unhappy customers your harshest and most vocal critics. I've also discovered that providing an excellent customer experience—the sum total of a customer's interactions with an organization—can be the single best way to set your company apart from competitors.

During my career, I've worked with thousands of organizations across a broad range of industries, helping them improve the experience they provide to customers. Based on this work, I've developed a practical, straightforward approach to creating and delivering an exceptional customer experience. It is applicable to all kinds of organizations—private and public companies, nonprofits, government agencies, and academic institutions. Throughout the book, when I refer to a business, company, or organization, I am describing any entity that interacts with and serves others. Likewise, when I refer to a customer, I mean any individual or group—including consumers, citizens, constituents, and students—served by another organization.

In presenting this approach, I use examples from nine organizations that best demonstrate how to deliver exceptional customer experiences. My hope—and my reason for writing this book—is that you can apply some of the same methods to improve your organization's customer experience.

Greg Gianforte
CEO and Founder
RightNow Technologies
June 2008

Foreword
By Don Peppers and Martha Rogers, Ph.D.

Let's face it, customer-facing technologies present a great temptation to businesses, because of the tremendous amount of customer information now readily available. The urge to use that personal information to sell more things is almost palpable, and you see it every day in the way companies approach their marketing and sales strategies.

Rather than starting with the question of how the personal data provided by a customer can be used to improve the customer's life—by making the product more convenient, perhaps, or less costly, or more tailored, or by making the customer reviews more informative, or the blog discussion more interesting—the overwhelming majority of the businesses we've observed have been asking the question the other way around: How can we use this technology and the customer data it throws off to sell more stuff? How do *we* extract the most value from *them*?

The problem is that this is a view of technology through the wrong end of the telescope. If you see technology mostly as a way to sell more stuff, then you're probably going to end up destroying value for your business. But if you see technology as a way to improve the customer's life, then you'll probably also sell more stuff.

We have always been enthusiastic advocates for customer relationship management, which we often define simply as treating different customers differently. But it could be said that relationship management technologies are most often used by a company to secure a 360-degree view of the customer, while what a company really needs is to visualize what it's like to *be* the customer, with a 360-degree view of the company.

Managing a customer's experience requires you to see your business from the outside in, looking through the customer's eyes to see your products and services, rather than from the inside out, looking at your customer from the point of view of your products or services.

The real question, in other words, is whether you are more concerned with what you can get from your customer, or with what your customer can get from you. Our contention is that if you stay focused on how the customer experiences your brand, including product, service, and interaction, and if you constantly try to improve that customer experience, then you are more likely to be able to create a sustainable, profitable business.

If you agree with our assessment, then this is definitely the book for you. *Eight to Great* will provide you with enough ideas, advice and thought-starters to keep you busy improving your customer experience for years. If you find it difficult to agree with our assessment, however, then this book will be more difficult for you, but if you read it carefully it might be of even greater value, because you won't be able to get through it without getting your world rocked, big time.

Greg Gianforte has crammed this succinct book absolutely chock full of information, advice, tips, guidelines, and how-to instructions for creating a better, more rewarding experience for your customers. *Eight to Great* has to be one of the best deals ever, in terms of good-advice-per-word-written.

No matter how much advice you get, of course, delivering great customer service is still going to be hard work. Delivering it in a personalized way, so that your service is tailored to the different needs of different customers is even harder. And delivering personalized customer service while still making a profit for your business is more difficult still.

But it isn't impossible, and increasingly, customers demand it. What's more, the best customers—the highly valuable ones most worth having as customers in the first place—these are the ones who demand the most personalized and efficient services.

So if you plan to have a business not just for today but for next year, and the year after—if you have any kind of ambition that your business will be a long-term success—then sooner or later you're going to have to understand the principles in *Eight to Great*.

Might as well be sooner. Keep reading.

Don Peppers and Martha Rogers are the founders of Peppers & Rogers Group and co-authors of Rules to Break and Laws to Follow.

Eight to Great

Eight Steps to Delivering an Exceptional Customer Experience

Section I
The Customer Experience Imperative

Introduction

In the classic 1947 movie *Miracle on 34ᵗʰ Street*, Macy's Santa Claus begins sending customers to other stores to find the toys they need to fulfill their children's Christmas wishes. Initially, the store owner, Mr. Macy, is concerned—sending customers to competitors doesn't make sense to him, despite the fact that Macy's toy inventory is depleted. The wisdom of this unorthodox approach becomes clear when one customer tells Mr. Macy that by helping her find the right toy at the right time (Christmas), he's earned a customer for life.

In much the same way, organizations today can earn the loyalty of customers: by taking knowledge about those customers and translating it into positive experiences for them. If you can't make it easy and satisfying for people to do business with you, you'll quickly lose them to someone who can. When customers can take their business elsewhere by simply picking up the phone, clicking on a Web link, grabbing a different item off the shelf, or driving a few more minutes down the road, delivering a good customer experience is critical to retaining customers and sustaining your business.

Conversely, not caring for your customers can have a devastating effect on your business. In fact, a recent survey revealed that 80 percent of respondents said they would **never** return to an organization after a poor customer experience.[1]

---

1 Harris Interactive. "U.S. Customer Experience Report," August 2007.

Despite such alarming statistics, organizations typically spend more time developing products and services than strategizing how to better serve and interact with customers.

In today's fast-moving global markets, companies must look closely at how they interact with customers. By creating a richer and more satisfying customer experience than competitors—and other companies in general—businesses can grow, improve margins, and build significant brand equity.

This book explains how to deliver customer experiences that transform people into lifelong customers. It outlines eight steps any organization can take to create world-class customer experiences. These steps are based on the proven best practices of industry leaders across virtually every market category. They are as practical and straightforward as they are effective.

To help you understand how you can apply these steps to your company, I've included examples from a number of organizations that have mastered the approach and transformed the customer experience they offer:

- Black & Decker
- eHarmony
- Electronic Arts
- iRobot
- Nikon
- Orbitz
- Right Start
- Shaklee
- TomTom

For far too long, businesses have treated customers as if they were nothing more than records in a database. Like the characters in *Miracle on 34th Street*, however, today's customers expect to be treated thoughtfully, with both care and respect. By providing customers with great experiences, you'll not only win their loyalty, but also secure your organization's position in the new consumer-centric economy.

Chapter 1
Defining the Customer Experience

"If you want to prosper, let your customer prosper."
— Frédéric Bastiat

The customer experience comprises the total of all interactions a customer has with an organization, along with the perceptions he or she subsequently forms about that organization. It includes all marketing, sales, and service interactions. It encompasses exchanges that occur in person, over the phone, via the Internet, and through traditional mail. Each interaction offers an opportunity to learn more about the customer's needs and preferences and to strengthen the relationship. Information gathered through each exchange can be used to tailor products, services, and future interactions. If you fail to collect knowledge about the customer or you ignore what you've learned, you'll fail to meet his or her expectations during future interactions. You'll probably annoy the customer and possibly lose his or her business.

Consider the following examples:

* After buying and using a product, a customer, pleased with the purchase, takes time to register on the manufacturer's website, complete a survey about the buying experience, and provide demographic information. The customer also specifies the types of information he's interested in receiving and indicates a preference for contact by email only. Soon the customer is getting calls from the company's telemarketers, receiving several catalogs every week, and getting an overwhelming

number of emails—mainly about products that are of no interest to him.

- A customer visits a company's website for guidance on how to use certain product features. The customer follows the steps suggested, but is unsuccessful. The customer then phones the company, reaches an automated voice response system, and when prompted, provides the information requested. After listening to a lengthy list of options, none of which match her needs, the customer opts to speak with an agent. After a long wait, the customer reaches an agent, who asks her to repeat all of the information she's already provided, then suggests that the customer walk through the steps she's already tried. Desperate, the customer repeats the steps, with no success. The agent offers to transfer the customer to another department. Frustrated, the customer hangs up.

In both examples, the customer's reasons for contacting the company have nothing to do with poor product quality or dissatisfaction, and yet both experiences are likely to leave a less-than-positive impression of the company. Worse, they may negatively affect the customer's future decisions about doing additional business with the company. Had the customer been dealing with organizations that truly cared about the experiences they deliver, the interactions would have differed greatly:

- The customer, after buying a product, registers on the manufacturer's website and indicates a preference for email contact only. He receives an immediate thank-you from the company, along with a discount offer for product accessories. Periodically, the company contacts the customer, by email only, to notify him of new items of interest, based on the product originally purchased.

- The customer visits a company's website to learn how to use certain product features. The site offers detailed instructions, along with diagrams and video demonstrations. At any point, the customer has the option to contact the company to ask questions in real time, by phone or via online chat, or to request a call from a consultant within a few hours. The site also offers an online forum where the customer can connect with others who have purchased similar products.

In these examples, the relationship between a company and its customer is strengthened, independent of the merits of a particular product, pricing, or distribution strategy. The customer's impressions are probably positive. Delivering these types of positive customer interactions requires appropriate technology, processes, and policies, along with careful planning and thoughtful execution—as described in the following chapters.

Chapter 2
Why Delivering a Superior Customer Experience is an Urgent Issue

"The customer is the immediate jewel of our souls."
– Ralph Waldo Emerson

The Internet and the global marketplace have dramatically altered the way companies and customers interact. Today's customers have a vast range of choices, greater expectations, and more information than ever before. If dissatisfied, they can easily take their business elsewhere. Organizations that don't recognize and adapt to these dynamics will not survive in the highly competitive global market.

Customers have more choices

When business was strictly local, customers could do only limited comparison shopping. They might visit or call a few companies before making a buying decision. Or they might continue to do business with a company because few—if any—alternatives were available. While most companies treated customers with courtesy and fairness, the customer experience was not a critical competitive differentiator. Offering products at relatively reasonable prices was typically sufficient to attract and retain customers.

But when consumers have more choices, the customer experience becomes much more important. The Internet gives consumers access to a global marketplace offering unprecedented choice. With a click of the mouse, they can find another vendor offering a similar product at a comparable price. In fact, they may find a company offering a better product at a lower price. In addition, switching to another vendor is easy and typically costs little or nothing. Given these factors, a superior customer experience may be the most compelling reason for a customer to do business with your organization.

Customers have higher expectations
In the past, when people interacted with a relatively small number of companies, their expectations were not high. They appreciated a friendly greeting and a bit of personal attention but didn't expect much more.

Today, however, nearly everyone has interacted with an organization that uses personalization, proactive communications, or other tactics to differentiate its customer experience. As a result, most customers' expectations are substantially elevated. If one company replies to a customer's email within a few hours, that customer will soon expect others to do the same. If one company always contacts a customer to ask about his or her purchase experience, the customer will begin to wonder why others don't.

It doesn't matter whether customers have a positive experience with a competing company or with a company in an entirely different market. The impact on their expectations is the same. Companies are no longer compared only to others in the same industry—they are now compared to the very best organizations customers have ever encountered.

And customers' expectations will continue to rise as they interact with more companies that have made a serious commitment to delivering a great customer experience. Those that don't make a similar commitment will become less competitive in comparison to these leaders—even if the quality of their customer experience doesn't change.

Customers are communicating with other customers

In addition to creating more choice, the Internet has also empowered customers to more effectively communicate with one another and to more easily create communities of interest around companies, products, and issues. When today's consumers are disgruntled, they can quickly visit a number of websites, online forums, or Internet communities and let thousands or possibly millions of others know. Thus, today a single negative customer experience can have a tremendously harmful effect on a company's reputation and brand image.

At the same time, the Web can amplify positive "buzz" about organizations that deliver exceptional customer experiences. Word-of-mouth advertising and viral marketing are much more powerful in today's digitally connected marketplace. As a result, the benefits of providing a consistently superb customer experience can be far greater today than they were even a few years ago.

Globalization has weakened price- and feature-based differentiation

Today, sustaining competitive differentiation based primarily on price is extremely difficult. Chances are good that somewhere in the world, another company can offer lower prices, and consumers can easily find that company using Web pricing comparison sites.

Sustaining differentiation based on product features is also challenging. Competitors can draw on the best talent from around the world to innovate and leapfrog one another in terms of product design and development. To further complicate the competitive landscape, technological innovations continuously compress time to market, enabling companies to respond to others' innovations with lightning speed.

When listing reasons for doing business with a company, customers rank service above quality and price.
While offering a good product at a competitive price is essential for attracting customers, it doesn't guarantee a sustainable competitive advantage. Today, customer loyalty is more likely to be driven by the quality of the experience than by price or product quality alone.

In fact, respondents in a recent study cited "outstanding service" as the number one reason they'd give more business to one company versus another—ahead of both "lowest price" and "best quality."[2]

Consumers who shop primarily based on price or who always want the latest bells and whistles will quickly switch to another vendor to get what they're looking for. But most people want to do business with companies that understand their individual needs and consistently demonstrate dedication to meeting those needs before **and** after a sale—companies devoted to delivering superior customer experiences.

Keeping customers is more profitable than finding new ones
Most companies know that attracting new customers is expensive, yet many tend to focus more on customer acquisition than on customer retention. As a result, they lose customers almost as quickly as they gain them—requiring them to continuously devote resources to costly customer acquisition initiatives.

---

2   Harris Interactive. "U.S. Customer Experience Report," August 2007.

This cycle of spending, acquiring, and losing customers is especially problematic in today's market, as customers can take their business elsewhere at the slightest provocation.

In contrast, companies that deliver outstanding customer experiences are able to break out of this unprofitable cycle by developing stronger bonds with their customers. These companies retain customers by keeping them satisfied. As a result, they don't have to spend as much on acquiring new customers—and they realize greater lifetime revenue from each customer they do acquire. This formula leads to steadier growth and greater profitability.

For these reasons, organizations of all sizes in all markets are recognizing that the customer experience can be a critical, strategic advantage. If a company does not treat customers in accordance with their expectations, those customers will find a company that does. Likewise, if constituents don't receive the service and attention they expect, they will rebel. If you can exceed customers' expectations, losing them to competitors is unlikely—even if those competitors offer lower prices or more advanced products.

In the global marketplace, customer experience wins, hands down. The trick is to translate intent and commitment into actions that actually satisfy, impress, and retain your customers.

Chapter 3
Why Most Organizations Have Failed to Provide a Superior Customer Experience

"As soon as you turn your back, you've lost your customer."
– Estée Lauder

Customers are increasingly dissatisfied with the way they are treated and are very vocal about their dissatisfaction. In fact, a survey conducted in August 2007 revealed that 94 percent of respondents said they'd had a negative customer experience, and 23 percent said that their experiences with **all** organizations over the past five years had been negative.[3]

That's quite a sweeping indictment, in light of the investments many companies have made in customer relationship management (CRM) software and other technology, which should be making interactions easier and more satisfying for customers—not making them more frustrating.

A brief examination of customer-related business and technology strategies highlights where organizations have gone wrong.

The myth of the "managed" relationship
One problem stems from the notion of customer relationship management. Most consumers don't want to be "managed," and they may resent the implication that their relationships with companies can be manipulated.

---

[3]   Harris Interactive. "U.S. Customer Experience Report," August 2007.

Many CRM technology initiatives are undertaken with little regard to customers' wants and needs. Instead they are focused on improving internal processes and driving cost savings. As a result, many organizations end up with systems that generate efficiencies in selling and servicing processes at the expense of long-term customer relationships and goodwill. This internally driven approach leads to behaviors that result in less-than-positive customer experiences.

An approach that is driven by customers' needs and preferences demonstrates that an organization values the customer relationship. In short, to satisfy customers, you have to let **them** manage **you**.

Frontline employees don't have the right resources
Another shortcoming of many CRM initiatives is that they are overly focused on supporting management rather than on empowering frontline staff. These initiatives, which typically require significant investments in technology, do enable management to track and analyze customer data and identify opportunities and emerging trends.

But because the battle for the customer is typically won or lost on the front line, employees who interact with customers—those who answer calls, draft customer communications, handle chat sessions, or reply to emails—need tools and information that help them better serve customers. These employees are the true face of a company, yet many companies fail to adequately provide them with the information and resources needed to address customers' issues and concerns effectively. As a result, customers are routinely sub-jected to experiences that send them to competitors.

The (dis)satisfaction survey

Many organizations use surveys to identify and address cus-tomer satisfaction issues, and typically conduct them once or twice each year. Survey results can help companies discover deficits in their customer experience and can enable them to track customer satisfaction scores over time.

The problem with periodic surveys is that they don't uncover customers' problems in time to quickly correct them and en-sure long-term loyalty. In fact, many dissatisfied customers won't complete a survey received months after a negative ex-perience, though they have no qualms about telling others about their dissatisfaction.

A better approach is to solicit customer input at the time of an interaction—at the "moment of truth," such as immedi-ately after a customer receives a new product or completes a customer service interaction. At these times, customers are often willing to offer their feedback—and intervention, if needed, is still possible.

Perhaps the main reason that companies are having trouble satisfying their customers is because it's difficult. Customers can be unreasonably demanding, frontline staff frequently turn over, and training new employees takes time. Companies often have limited budgets that prevent them from making the changes needed to ensure a consistently satisfying cus-tomer experience. Delivering outstanding service requires a close orchestration of people, processes, and technology; the agility to respond quickly to change; and a customer-centric company culture.

Despite these challenges, certain organizations continue to deliver superior customer experiences. These companies prioritize the customer experience and manage it effectively. As a result, many of them have emerged as market leaders. Their examples are instructive to anyone who wants to understand what it takes to deliver a remarkable customer experience.

Chapter 4
Why Delivering a Superior Customer Experience is a Worthwhile Investment

"The only profit center is the customer."
— Peter Drucker

Because most organizations today must address numerous challenges with limited resources, many may question whether the customer experience should be a prioritized investment.

The answer is a resounding "Yes!" Organizations in virtually every industry have reaped the benefits of a differentiated customer experience. From consumer products and financial services companies to government agencies and educational institutions, these organizations have demonstrated that deliberate, systematic improvements in the quality of customer interactions pay significant dividends.

Organizations that doubt the real value of a customer experience initiative need only consider some of the research that links customer satisfaction levels to profitability. For example, a study by Purdue University revealed that customer satisfaction was a strong indicator of downstream profitability.[4] In fact, comparing customer satisfaction to profitability has become an accepted business metric. Two former Harvard Business School professors proved a direct link between superior service experiences, customer loyalty, and a company's financial performance.[5] Although the

---

4   "Purdue research links employee satisfaction, profits," September 13, 2004: http://www.purdue.edu/UNS/html4ever/2004/040913.Oakley.sat.html.
5   Mackey, Jack, "Putting the Service Profit Chain to Work," December 29, 2004: http://www.franchising.com/articles/51/.

benefits of delivering exceptional customer experiences can vary, they are consistently substantial. A few prime examples follow.

Improve customer experience while controlling costs

When the fast-growing multinational company TomTom launched its innovative personal navigation product line, it faced numerous obstacles to market acceptance. One of the biggest was breaking out of the "gadget lover" demographic and into the mainstream consumer market, which is largely technophobic. In strategizing about how to tap into the consumer market, the company decided to prioritize the customer experience.

The company had traditionally used an email-based system to manage communications with customers and had posted conventional frequently asked questions (FAQs) on its website. As business grew, these channels proved insufficient, particularly during the holiday season when a backlog of emails and long phone queues threatened customer satisfaction. When a subsequent product upgrade elicited a huge market response, which TomTom was unequipped to handle, the company recognized the need to enhance its customer service operations.

TomTom empowered its frontline employees to listen to customers and act on what they learned during customer interactions. The company also implemented an online self-service system that gives customers immediate access to a wide range of information. Analytics and reporting tools provide employees with visibility into customers' changing needs, enabling the company to frequently update information on its website in response to those needs. On average, the system handles more than two million customer questions every month, which has helped limit the volume of incoming email and phone calls, despite rapidly increasing product sales, evidenced by an 800 percent increase in revenue. Most important, the company has been able to achieve high levels of customer satisfaction while controlling operational costs.

Personalized customer experience

Despite the strength of Nikon's brand, the company faces significant competition in the digital camera market. Compared to Nikon, other consumer electronics companies have greater manufacturing economies of scale, stronger presence in worldwide distribution channels, and higher tolerance of slim margins because of other profitable product lines. To fend off competitors, Nikon made a board-level commitment to providing a differentiated customer experience. It carefully segmented its market and developed value-added loyalty programs to create a deeply personalized customer experience.

Nikon implemented its customer experience initiative in phases. Contact center employees were provided with an online knowledge foundation that helps them respond quickly to customers' needs. To facilitate online self-service, a subset of this internal technical knowledge base was made available through a public website. After enhancing the company's website capabilities, Nikon replaced its existing email and call-tracking systems with a state-of-the-art integrated solution. One of the greatest gains has been the speed with which Nikon staff can respond to and address customers' issues. The system enables Nikon contact center staff to view customers' complete service histories across all contact points—including telephone, website, email, and fax—so they can provide effective, personalized support. It also allows incidents to be quickly routed or escalated to the most appropriate staff member across various locations and tiers. And it enables Nikon staff and customers to find current, relevant answers to common questions with just a few keystrokes. The knowledge foundation and multichannel contact system, available in nineteen languages, is used by Nikon employees and customers in fifty countries, which helps to ensure that the company delivers a consistently excellent customer experience worldwide. Even as the company's sales volume continues to grow, Nikon consistently scores over 95 percent in customer satisfaction surveys.

TomTom and Nikon are examples of how a differentiated customer experience can improve business performance; other examples are described later in this book. Some companies have found that their investments in the customer experience pay off by improving conversion rates on their e-commerce sites. Others see increases in their up-sell and cross-sell activity. Universities see enrollments rise; government agencies satisfy constituents and more effectively fulfill their legislative mandates.

The ultimate motivation for investing in the customer experience, however, may be the consequences of **not** doing so. Companies that don't commit sufficient resources to a customer experience initiative typically encounter one or more of the following problems:

- Higher customer defection
- Decline in market share
- Downward pressure on pricing
- Drop in market awareness and word-of-mouth referrals

- Rise in contact center costs
- Reduction in sales staff productivity

The following chapters lay out eight steps that can help any organization avoid these problems and deliver a richly satisfying customer experience.

Section II
Eight Steps to Customer Experience Success

"Find purpose. The means will follow."

– Mahatma Gandhi

Introduction

Once you make the decision to differentiate your company's customer experience, you need to determine where to start. To identify areas where improvements can be most quickly made, you need to assess your organization's strengths and weaknesses. This review is essential because most organizations don't have a realistic view of the customer experience they provide. In a recent survey of companies and their customers, only 8 percent of customers described their experience as "superior," while 80 percent of the companies believed the customer experience they were providing was superior.[6] Such a disparity in perception indicates the need for baselining your customer experience.

The customer experience scorecard

The following scorecard can be helpful in quantifying your organization's current customer experience; it will also help to highlight areas that most need attention and improvement. Based on your own company's goals, you will need to determine and apply the most appropriate metrics. For example, many contact center managers try to minimize talk time to increase agent productivity—the faster agents end

---

6   Meyer, Christopher, and Andrew Schwager. "Understanding Customer Experience," *Harvard Business Review*, February 2007.

21

calls, the better. But for organizations that implement Web and voice self-service technologies, tracking call duration may not be the best way to assess progress. If customers can solve simple problems without assistance, agents will handle more complicated issues, and talk times are likely to increase rather than decrease. In this case, a more appropriate metric is call volume, which should decrease once customers use self-service options.

To demonstrate how the scorecard can be used, the following example assesses a fictitious company's performance and should help to provide a starting point.

The Eight steps to delivering a great customer experience
You can apply the following steps to successfully differentiate your company's customer experience:

- **Step One:** Establish a knowledge foundation.
- **Step Two:** Empower customers with self-service.
- **Step Three:** Empower frontline staff.
- **Step Four:** Offer multichannel choice.
- **Step Five:** Listen to your customers.
- **Step Six:** Design seamless experiences.
- **Step Seven:** Engage proactively with customers.
- **Step Eight**: Measure and improve continuously.

Score assessment:
40–50: Ready to implement strategies for continuous improvement
30–39: Targeted improvements required
0–29: Broad improvements required

	Strongly Agree: 5	Agree: 4	Neutral: 3	Disagree: 2	Strongly Disagree: 1	Score
Our customers are empowered to help themselves when they need information from us.		X				4
Customers can conveniently contact us via the channel of their choice (voice, email, online, chat).			X			3
Regardless of how customers contact us, they will receive the same answer to the same question.			X			3
When a customer calls, we know whether he or she has recently received a promotional email from us.			X			3
Customers can track and view their interactions (order history, service incidents, account status).		X				4
Our employees have a single view of all customer interactions, regardless of type.			X			3
When we engage with our customers, we provide them with relevant, personalized information.	X					5
We capture the voice of the customer by proactively seeking feedback, and we take immediate action when necessary.			X			3
We continually exceed our service goals (first-call resolution rate, service-level agreements).				X		2
We help connect our customers with one another by offering events, communities, or forums.					X	1
TOTAL						31

Customer Experience Assessment Scorecard

After assessing the quality of your company's current customer experience, you're ready to start planning the first stage of a customer experience initiative.

Avoid the pitfalls

Because the customer experience is influenced by many types of interactions across many touch points, companies often make the mistake of defining their initial projects too broadly. By undertaking a project that is too large, they often fail to deliver the quantifiable, near-term results that justify continued investments in improving the customer experience.

Another error companies frequently make is to design customer interactions based strictly on internal drivers. They approach the customer experience in terms of what **they** want customers to do and how **they** can influence customer behavior in the most cost-effective way, instead of considering what customers want and need. A third common mistake is overreliance on technology or process change to bring about needed improvements. The following guidelines should help you avoid these common pitfalls.

- *Take a staged, incremental approach:* Focusing on areas where improvements can be made most quickly will help you deliver near-term results and build credibility with key decision makers. This approach will help in securing the support of frontline staff, department heads, and other pivotal constituencies—an essential factor in building a truly transformed, customer-centric business culture.

- *Adhere rigorously to the customer's perspective:* Improvements to the customer experience begin when you focus on customers' wants and needs. Meeting these needs may require changes in both business processes and organizational structure. Project teams must consider all company/customer interactions from the customer's perspective and must make changes based on what is most appealing to the customer.

- *Adopt the right technologies along with proven best practices:* Technology, in conjunction with new processes and policies, designed around customer expectations is the optimal combination for achieving success.

- *Maintain a proactive—rather than reactive—mindset:* Creating a corporate culture that fosters the behaviors and decisions that result in an outstanding customer experience is essential. To significantly improve your company's customer experience, employees must approach the customer experience with a proactive mindset. Answering questions before customers ask, providing customers with information before they need it, or personalizing communications based on previous interactions are all examples of exceptional customer service.

Based on the real-world successes of thousands of organizations around the world, these steps define specific areas where you can focus your efforts for maximum benefit. Applying the lessons learned by these organizations will enable you to benefit from their customer experience initiatives before undertaking your own project. By focusing on the specific, achievable goals outlined in these steps, you can radically enhance your company's customer experience while laying the groundwork for further improvements. You can also use this material to present a credible roadmap to key decision makers whose support is essential in transforming the way your organization does business.

Each of these eight focus areas can help your company and your customers realize all the tangible, high-impact benefits that accompany such improvements. These steps are presented in the following chapters in an order that yields dramatic results.

Chapter 1
Establish a Knowledge Foundation

"An investment in knowledge always pays the best interest."
– Benjamin Franklin

Have you ever phoned a company and spoken with a friendly representative who is no help at all? He doesn't know your order history or account balance and can't answer any of your questions about product features, return policies, or warranties. The only assistance the rep provides is offering to transfer you to someone else.

Unfortunately, we all know that this type of experience is far too common. These interactions that frequently frustrate consumers are also costly for companies, as poor service often results in customer defections. Fortunately, the solution is straightforward: provide the right knowledge, to the right person, at the right time. Because lack of knowledge is at the root of most negative customer experiences, the first step in delivering an exceptional customer experience is establishing a knowledge foundation. A knowledge foundation is the platform on which you will deliver consistent, rewarding experiences to your customers.

A knowledge foundation should be easily accessible by employees and customers alike. Employees will use it as a source of information that will help them enhance customer interactions. Customers will use the knowledge foundation through a variety of self-service options (which are described in the next chapter).

Your knowledge foundation should contain two primary types of knowledge. The first is knowledge about your products, services, and company. Think of this knowledge as answers to your customers' questions. The second type is knowledge about your customers. Examples include demographics, past purchases, interaction history, and explicit and implicit preferences. Armed with this knowledge, employees will be well equipped to deliver a great customer experience.

Best practices for building a knowledge foundation

Contrary to the opinion of many experts, establishing an effective knowledge foundation does not need to be a resource-intensive exercise. You should avoid manually assembling and maintaining a knowledge foundation because this approach is both time-consuming and expensive. And manual methods typically result in a collection of poorly organized information that reflects what subject matter experts believe is important, not what customers want or need. Also, without continuous monitoring and revisions, the information quickly becomes outdated. Instead of attempting to manually assemble your knowledge foundation, take advantage of solutions that automate the collection, dissemination, and updating of information.

Choose a knowledge foundation solution

To fulfill the knowledge requirements of a differentiated customer experience, many organizations must shift their approach to how knowledge is collected, directed, and maintained. Consider the breakthrough approaches of eBay and YouTube. Conventional wisdom would have directed eBay to have employees monitor sellers' auctions and post-sale service; instead, eBay lets buyers rank and review the quality of sellers' merchandise and service. Likewise, YouTube could have employees view postings to ensure quality control and rank them according to their preferences. Instead, YouTube videos are ranked by viewers—the more a video is viewed, the higher it is posted. eBay and YouTube both displayed a common stroke of genius by putting power in the hands of their customers.

Take advantage of self-learning technologies

Creating an effective knowledge foundation should be no different. You probably have thousands of customers interacting with you daily through your website, email, chat, and the phone. Let them suggest the content and assess its quality for you. This approach, combined with the right self-learning technology, will guarantee that your knowledge foundation is what your customers want, is always up to date, and dynamically adjusts to changing customer needs.

Look for self-learning technology that applies advanced artificial intelligence (AI) techniques to automate the building and maintenance of a knowledge foundation. You don't need to understand how AI works—just that it provides tremendous benefits in streamlining the creation and maintenance of a knowledge foundation. When selecting a knowledge foundation solution, look for one that incorporates some or all of the following AI techniques:

- **Bayesian learning** is a computational learning technique that finds patterns in data using co-occurrence probabilities, so that systems can be more helpful by accurately predicting what knowledge will be useful.

- **Biomimicry** makes your knowledge foundation smarter by imitating nature's best designs and processes, based on the principle that nature has already solved many human problems.

- **Clustering** is a data analysis technique that partitions a data set into subsets (clusters) whose elements share common traits.

- **Collaborative filtering** makes automatic predictions (filtering) about the needs or interests of a user by collecting taste information from many users (collaborative). Relevant information is brought to the attention of a user by observing patterns in previous behaviors and comparing those to behaviors and patterns of many other users.

- **Natural language processing (NLP)** refers to a computer system's ability to understand human (natural) language. NLP techniques include identifying and correcting misspellings and identifying (and then ignoring) frequently occurring words such as *the, in, of,* and *on,* which improves search results.

- **Neural network** is a computational learning technique that automatically finds patterns. It is loosely modeled on the functional workings of biological neurons. A self-organizing map is a type of neural network used to cluster information. It can generate maps of an information landscape, keeping conceptually similar items in close proximity to one another, which enables a visual interpretation of data.

- **Self organizing system** is a term used to describe the use of any of a number of approaches, such as neural networks, swarm intelligence, or Bayesian learning, to create a learning system. The term usually connotes the display and access of the data in the system as occurring in some logical, but evolving manner. For example, a retailer's gift-wrapping information should automatically be made more visible before holidays, while return/exchange information should be more visible during post-holiday periods.

- **Swarm intelligence** is a computational learning technique of finding patterns in data. It is loosely based on the concept of multiple entities competing for resources in a limited-resource environment. The entities quickly identify the relevant bits of information and can rapidly change to new information once that information becomes more relevant.

- **Automatic usefulness ranking** is the process of positioning items in relation to their relevance or helpfulness to others. For example, an Internet search engine may rank pages according to an evaluation of their relevance, making it possible for a user to quickly select pages that they are likely to want to see.

These techniques enable you to continuously build content based on the questions customers actually ask, so that your knowledge foundation is always closely aligned with your customers' real-world needs. They also virtually eliminate the time-consuming, expensive, and error-prone manual processes associated with traditional knowledge management. The business result of a self-learning system is that the more useful information automatically becomes more visible to employees and customers.

In addition to these AI techniques, an effective knowledge foundation should have the following capabilities:

- **Scheduled knowledge review:** To ensure that the information in your knowledge foundation is current, you should be able to assign an expiration date to each piece of stored information. On the expiration date, your knowledge foundation should automatically trigger a review of the information so that any required updates or corrections can be made.

- **Knowledge effectiveness reporting:** You must continually monitor how your knowledge foundation is used. Look for a solution that automatically tracks and reports on the information that customers and employees search for, what content is provided to them, and whether or not that content was helpful. For example, a standard knowledge foundation effectiveness report should show what terms customer are searching, how many times those terms were searched, and how many answers are available for each term.

- **Language support:** If your company does business internationally—or plans to—you should confirm that your knowledge foundation supports translation into the various languages you'll need.

- **Access for users with disabilities:** Your organization may need to provide access to visually or physically impaired users to comply with government regulations. For example, in the United States, Section 508 requires all federal agencies to ensure that their information technology takes into account the needs of all end users, including people with disabilities.

- **Knowledge authoring tools:** Your self-learning system should be able to indicate areas where more content is needed and should provide capabilities to author and properly classify content. Look for an integrated knowledge-authoring environment that is easy to use and allows robust formatting, such as WYSIWYG HTML.

- **Taxonomy:** As you author knowledge items, you will need the ability to create a taxonomy of your information in order to classify items by product line, customer usage, or other categories. Over time, different portions of the taxonomy will be maintained by different groups within your organization. Be sure that any system you select supports robust, multilayer organizing taxonomies for your knowledge items and associated ownership models; also, ensure that single knowledge items can be assigned to multiple categories. For example, you do not want to maintain separate warranty knowledge items for each product if the warranty information applies to all your products. You want to be able to assign the warranty knowledge items to all product categories, without duplicating the information.

- **Knowledge segmentation:** You may need the ability to segment knowledge so that certain users can view only portions of your content. For example, if your organization sells through distributors, you may want to share updates about products and pricing with them, but not with customers.

- **Knowledge approval routing:** Most larger organizations have procedures for approving information released to employees and customers. Be sure that any system you select provides workflow automation to support your approval processes.

- **Explicit knowledge placement:** You're bound to have emergency situations when you need to get information to customers quickly. Any solution you select should allow you to publish content in minutes and to automatically make it highly visible.

- **Robust knowledge types:** Because a picture is often worth a thousand words, be sure that any knowledge system you select supports multimedia knowledge items such as embedded videos, flash demos, and animation. Also, knowledge items should be able to attach a variety of file formats, because many organizations have information such as applications, registrations, and marketing brochures in Adobe PDF or Microsoft Word format. The content of attachments should be searchable by someone using the knowledge foundation.

- **Indexing of external information:** Often you'll need to provide access to files and information that might not be stored in the knowledge foundation itself, so look for a system that you can direct to search and index information stored elsewhere on your corporate network. When a user conducts a search, both items stored in the knowledge foundation and external data should be retrieved.

How to build a self-learning knowledge foundation
If you have selected the right technology, beginning to build an effective knowledge foundation is simple and straightforward. The following steps should help:

- **Seed:** Quickly establish your knowledge foundation by seeding it with a limited number of questions and answers. Don't try to load everything but the kitchen sink. Start with basic information, and add content over time. A good way to determine what information is needed is to spend an afternoon in your contact center listening to agents. You'll find that they spend most time answering basic questions. Use those questions and answers as the starting point for your knowledge foundation. You'll quickly discover that a small amount of information addresses a wide range of customer inquiries and needs. Initially, seed the knowledge foundation with thirty (or fewer) question-and-answer pairs; later you can add more.

- **Capture:** Use the self-learning capabilities of your system to determine where gaps exist in your knowledge foundation, based on actual customer interactions. Every question that is submitted via your website or via email points to potential information gaps where additional content is needed. Capture agents' responses to these questions and route them for possible approval and publishing. The key is to learn what customers want and need—and to expand the available information accordingly. By continuously applying this step, you'll keep your knowledge foundation fresh as new products are introduced and customer interests change over time.

- **Organize:** Businesses tend to organize knowledge based on attributes such as product lines and locations. Customers, however, often think in terms of product uses or types of problems. Organizing information for easy access is the most critical step in building your knowledge foundation. Fortunately, this complex task is handled automatically by the self-learning AI capabilities intrinsic to your foundation. Useful knowledge becomes more visible, and chaff is automatically made less visible or removed.

Ensure deliverability across the front lines of your business
A knowledge system by itself is much like Einstein's brain without a body: smart, but of little use. To drive business value, your knowledge foundation must be connected directly to the business applications across all the customer touch channels in your business (email, Web, phone, interactive voice response, agent desktop, and chat). The specifics of this approach are described in later chapters.

As you select a knowledge foundation, it is essential that you keep an eye toward the customer channels that will be most important to your business now and in the future. Failure to do so will leave you with a potentially very smart but disconnected island of knowledge that drives little business value.

Leverage all appropriate resources
Although a knowledge foundation should encompass many types of information, it doesn't have to reside in a single, monolithic system. Building and maintaining such a system could be prohibitively expensive—and would likely require the abandonment of useful business applications. Rather than overhauling your company's IT environment, imple-

ment an open knowledge foundation that can leverage a full range of data sources—including CRM databases, return merchandise authorization (RMA) systems, Web content, transaction processing systems, online bulletin boards, business intelligence applications, and other relevant information resources.

Integrating applications and other systems with your knowledge foundation allows you to take advantage of previous IT investments and broaden the scope of knowledge in the foundation.

A robust, well-automated knowledge foundation is essential for supporting a differentiated customer experience. The best way to begin realizing quantifiable business value from a knowledge foundation is to follow Step Two—empowering customers with self-service capabilities—which is covered in the next chapter.

Doing It Right: iRobot

Goals:
- Maximize adoption of products by providing an excellent customer experience.
- Optimize use of online communication channels.
- Control costs.

The Challenge: Serving a broad customer base
iRobot, maker of the Roomba® Vacuum Cleaning Robots, serves a rapidly growing, very diverse customer base. Because many of iRobot's customers are not tech-savvy, the company needs to answer their questions quickly, clearly, and accurately.

The Solution: A self-learning knowledge foundation
iRobot selected a customer service tool that features a unique self-learning knowledge foundation. The knowledge foundation provides a dynamically updated list of the most commonly asked questions, ensuring that a maximum number of users can find the information they need without initiating a search. It also suggests to the company areas for improvement based on customer questions and feedback. To make the knowledge foundation as helpful as possible, iRobot augments text answers with pictures and video clips.

Customers can find answers to their questions on the iRobot website within minutes. As a result, 97 percent of customer inquires are handled via Web self-service, and iRobot has seen significant decreases in email and phone volumes despite rapid sales growth.

Contact center employees have access to the same knowledge foundation and also have instant access to the customer's interaction history and past queries. This enables them to answer customer queries quickly and consistently, while sparing customers from having to repeat information as they cross interaction channels.

Achievements:

- Of customers seeking information, 97 percent find what they need on iRobot's website.
- A unified view of customer feedback from monthly customer surveys is used to enhance products and service.
- Graphics and video on the website assist customers in using products.

Chapter 2
Empower Customers with Self-Service

"If you ever need a helping hand, you'll find one at the end of your arm."
– Audrey Hepburn

One of the most powerful—and immediately rewarding—ways to improve the customer experience is to expose your knowledge foundation to customers through effective self-service mechanisms, such as on the Web or with voice self-service. By providing customers with easy, direct access to your knowledge foundation, you enable them to find the information they need whenever they want it. Many companies have found that by offering self-service options to customers they improve customer satisfaction because many customers want the convenience of self-service options that are available 24-7.

Benefits of a self-service approach
Self-service options can significantly improve the service that contact centers provide. Customers can usually find needed information much faster via Web self-service or integrated voice self-service than they can if they opt to speak with an agent. At the same time, when customers choose self-service options, call volumes decrease, giving agents more time for complex questions and personalized service, which enhances the customer experience.

An intelligent knowledge foundation combined with best practices for continuously fine-tuning the self-service system can generate self-service rates (the percentage of customers who contact your organization for information and are able to find it without personal attention) of 85 percent or higher.

With these self-service rates, incoming emails are often reduced by 30 to 50 percent and calls by 10 to 15 percent.

Additional benefits of self-service, for both customers and your company, can include:

- **Speed:** Self-service enables customer to find information immediately, without waiting for an email response or for a call center agent.

- **Round-the-clock service:** Many organizations can't afford to operate a 24-hour contact center, yet consumers frequently need and expect help during evenings and weekends. Self-service ensures that help is available whenever customers need it.

- **Effectiveness:** Diagrams, photos, and video clips can be extremely helpful to customers looking for assistance. They usually find these types of resources—when available through self-service options—more convenient and helpful than live assistance.

- **Relief for other channels:** An effective self-service environment can reduce the workloads of agents, employees, or partners who assist customers and can enable them to spend more time with customers requiring personal attention—which can lead to dramatic improvements in the overall customer experience.

- **True first-contact resolution:** Many consumers check websites for answers before contacting a company. By providing Web self-service options, companies can ensure that customers find what they need the first time they seek assistance.

- **Rich market insight:** Customers' use of self-service systems can provide visibility into their preferences and buying patterns. By tracking customers' self-service actions, you can gather information that can help personalize future offers, improve product and service offerings, and further differentiate your customer experience.

  For example, the customer support group at Electronic Arts (EA) provides game developers with customer feedback that helps them improve game design and predict potential issues with new games—all prior to product launch, which results in a vastly improved customer experience.

- **Cost savings:** Each phone call handled by contact center staff is estimated to cost between $3 and $15.[7] A recent benchmark cites an average cost of $2.70 to $5.60 per call for large organizations, and $6 to $8 per call for smaller companies.[8] The average cost of responding to a single email can range from about $1 to $40.[9] By offloading these interactions to Web and voice self-service systems, which cost pennies per contact, companies routinely save millions.

- **Scalability:** Businesses can experience significant spikes in contact center traffic due to seasonal cycles, new

---

7   Sweeney, Terry. "Answering the call," FCW.com, August 22, 2005: http://www.fcw.com/print/11_32/news/90269-1.html

8   Barry, Curt. "Managing Your Cost Per Call," Multichannel Merchant.com, January 30, 2007: http://multichannelmerchant.com/opsandfulfillment/contact_center_advisor/cost_percall/index.html

9   Barkai, Joe. "Benchmarking in Call Centers," October 21, 2003.

product releases, product defects, and other causes. Staffing up the contact center to deal with sudden peaks in demand can be costly and impractical. Web and voice self-service, in comparison, can scale to handle large numbers of interactions without additional staff.

Building world-class self-service
Selecting a self-service solution

By now, you should be convinced of the value of offering self-service options. As you begin to evaluate available solutions, use the following capabilities checklist:

- **Ease of use:** With Web self-service, customers should have several ways of finding the information they seek—including keyword searches, natural-language queries, and browsing by category. Make sure that customers can always access self-service options with one click, from anywhere on your website. The hyperlink that directs them to your self-service options should be labeled consistently and in the same location on each page. Also, context-sensitive links should be available throughout the site. Your solution should be able to automatically maintain a "Top 10" list of the most commonly sought answers by topic area, which should be prominently posted on your website. Many customers will find what they need with a single mouse click.

- **Simple escalation processes:** Customers using self-service features should always be able to quickly escalate problems to a company representative. Escalation options should include chat, email, a scheduled call with a company representative, or the posting of a question on a Web forum. Without escalation options within your self-service system, customers may become frustrated and less likely to use self-service in the future.

- **Multilingual support:** For effective self-service, you must communicate with customers in their native languages. Translating customer-facing portions of a knowledge foundation into multiple languages is more cost-effective than having multilingual contact center staff. Be sure that your solution can support your current and future language needs.

Implementing effective self-service

Once you have selected a self-service solution, use the following guidelines to ensure that your system is effective.

- **Start small:** Because a large percentage of customers' questions are typically related to a relatively small set of issues, self-service can be extremely effective even with a limited amount of knowledge content. Don't wait to get started. Post the knowledge you know will be useful, and then use the self-learning capabilities of your knowledge foundation to augment and improve.

- **Continuously fine-tune:** Companies that are most successful with self-service are diligent about managing and fine-tuning their systems. They review keyword reports to ensure that all search terms used by customers have adequate content associated with them and that search terms don't return an overwhelming amount of content. They collect and evaluate customer feedback about specific content to see if it can be more clearly worded or supplemented with graphics or other visual aids. They also typically take steps to drive traffic to self-service options by highlighting these options on the website, mentioning them in on-hold phone messages, and referring to them in printed product materials.

- **Use the customer's language:** In addition to communicating with customers in their native languages, conveying information in the simplest way is also important. Avoid highly technical terms, industry jargon, or slang. Self-service information should be conveyed in such a way that new customers, with little knowledge of your products or services, can understand and benefit from the information.

For example, when iRobot recognized that a number of its vacuum robots were purchased by customers who weren't tech-savvy, the company enhanced its knowledge foundation with visual content. It combined material from product manuals with pictures and video clips to make its self-service information clearer and easier to understand for these users.

With voice self-service, allow customers to navigate the system using both touch-tone inputs and spoken words. Today's speech recognition technology can enable customers to perform searches by phone that are as effective as Web searches and will appeal to customers who aren't Internet-savvy.

Encouraging customers to use self-service options
In promoting self-service channels, be sure to offer customers a range of choices for interaction, and don't forget to include ways for customers to quickly escalate issues or reach

live support. Any of the following methods can help to drive certain customer interactions to lower-cost, self-service channels:

- **Make online self-service links prominent** on your website, and always offer self-service options first or at the same time that you offer a customer support phone number or email address.

- **Integrate online help** throughout key processes such as purchases or returns.

- **Promote Web and voice self-service resources** in the messages customers hear while they're on hold.

- **Have call center agents notify customers of self-service options** and, if needed, provide instructions on how to use them.

- **Accept questions from customers via Web forms** that can be used to direct customers to appropriate self-service content.

- **Reply to emails with a hyperlink** to appropriate self-service content, instead of providing a complete answer by email.

Measuring self-service effectiveness

To gauge the effectiveness of self-service options, you need to determine self-service rates. To do so, track the total number of self-service sessions on your site and compare this with the number of visitors who escalate issues to the contact center by calling, submitting an email or Web form or initiating a chat session. If you implement voice self-service, monitor your success rate in a similar way. Many organizations have achieved Web self-service rates of 90 percent, and some have achieved rates as high as 99 percent, especially when most customers are asking routine questions.

Web and voice self-service can significantly improve your customer experience and substantially reduce your costs. You can't stop there, however, because much of your customer experience will still involve interactions between customers and the people on the front lines of your business. To fully optimize your customer experience, therefore, you must fully empower these frontline employees to fulfill your customers' needs and exceed their expectations. Step Three explores the process of empowering frontline staff, which is covered in the next chapter.

Doing It Right: Electronic Arts

Goals:
- Provide effective support to millions of customers worldwide, across hundreds of game titles.
- Handle rapidly growing incident volume with reduced budget.

The Challenge: Support global growth while maintaining cost-efficiency

Electronic Arts (EA), the world's leading independent producer of electronic games, with millions of customers all over the world, must provide outstanding customer service to maintain its competitive edge. As the company was experiencing a rapid increase in inquiries due to exploding global growth, the customer support operation was also forced to cut costs and staff.

The Solution: Self-service relieves crunch

Self-service is a critical component of EA's customer support strategy. EA's robust knowledge foundation empowers customers to easily find answers on the Web and via voice self-service. EA has also taken the innovative step of making the knowledge foundation available within online games, enabling customers to seek help without having to leave the game environment.

By offering self-service options, EA has been able to successfully handle a huge increase in inquiry volume with a decreased budget. In addition, EA's customer service staff can now focus on more complex inquiries that require a personal touch.

Achievements:
- Improved responsiveness by 20 percent.
- Improved customer satisfaction by 20 percent, while handling a 60 percent increase in incident volume and a 20 percent decrease in budget.

Chapter 3
Empower Frontline Staff

*"Knowledge is of two kinds: what we know ourselves
and where we know we can find out what we don't know."*
– Samuel Johnson

To provide outstanding customer experiences, frontline staff must always be able to provide customers with timely, relevant, and comprehensive assistance—and be empowered to resolve issues.

Without access to a knowledge foundation, customer-facing staff will be ill-equipped to address customer needs, and customers often interpret an employee's lack of knowledge as a sign that your company does not value their business. In addition, less-than-knowledgeable staff may aggravate unhappy customers by saying or doing the wrong thing.

By giving frontline employees easy access to your knowledge foundation, you'll empower them to answer customer questions promptly and accurately. With access to information about a customer's previous interactions with a company, employees can provide personalized assistance, demonstrate that they understand the customer's needs and preferences, and save customers from having to repeat themselves. They'll also be able to appropriately address any problems that may occur during the course of each customer's interactions with your company.

In addition to giving frontline employees access to your knowledge foundation, some practical ways to empower frontline staff with the knowledge needed to deliver a great customer experience include:

- **Interviewing veterans:** The most experienced frontline employees are typically familiar with the most common customer questions and information requests. By sharing their knowledge, you can better train and empower less experienced team members.

- **Enabling employees to update the knowledge foundation:** Because frontline employees typically have the most frequent contact with customers, they are aware of current issues and resolutions. Enabling them to propose changes to information in the knowledge foundation will ensure that the information is always current and relevant.

- **Using desktop real estate wisely:** You can boost frontline performance by optimizing the interface of desktop applications. When employees can click a tab or expand a field to access information, rather than open multiple applications, they'll serve customers faster.

- **Continuing to adapt:** Adjust knowledge resources to mirror changes in your business, such as providing relevant seasonal information or details about products recently introduced.

Who should be empowered with this knowledge?

Within most companies, multiple groups interact with customers and can benefit from access to your knowledge foundation. Because the majority of customer interactions will take place with contact center staff, start there. These employees typically have the most day-to-day contact with customers. They may be individuals who handle multiple tiers of escalation or subject-matter experts who typically address specific issues. Also, supervisors who manage frontline staff members need appropriate knowledge resources to make informed decisions about how to guide and improve the performance of their employees.

Taking an inventory of the various groups within your organization and learning how they work with customers will help you best address those customers' specific needs. In addition to contact center staff, consider these other employees:

- **Salespeople:** The sales team may include account representatives, in-store retail staff, website support, and in-house telesales teams.

- **Marketers:** This group interacts with customers through various events, campaigns, and communications.

- **Work-at-home agents:** More and more companies are employing work-at-home agents to tap into a broader workforce and cut costs.

- **Field support staff:** This group can include administrative and operations personnel, as well as IT and other specialized technical teams.

- **Outsourcers, independent dealers, and other third parties:** Those who have frontline contact with customers may not always be company employees. You may need to extend knowledge resources beyond the walls of your organization, to partners, distributors, or any group that provides services, products, or support to customers.

What knowledge do people need?

Too much information can be as problematic as too little. Information overload can make it difficult for employees to find the specific knowledge needed to enhance a customer interaction as it occurs. In a fast-paced environment, frontline employees don't have time to search and browse through irrelevant information. Thus, in addition to giving each frontline employee access to your knowledge foundation, it is essential to filter, prioritize, and proactively provide information based on actual need or request.

As you determine what information should be made available to frontline staff, consider the following:

- **Role:** Desktop workspaces should be tailored to each individual's role. For example, you should have one desktop configured for employees who are processing returns, and a different one for employees focused on new account initiatives.

- **Subject matter:** As soon as a frontline employee recognizes that an interaction relates to a particular subject—such as a product feature or a company policy—he or she should be able to immediately access relevant knowledge that is both directly and indirectly related to that subject.

- **Customer:** Regardless of role, any employee interacting with customers needs information about each customer with whom he or she is interacting. The customer's record should be automatically retrieved by software that recognizes a phone number or identifies an email address, and it should contain a history of all previous interactions the customer has had with your organization, regardless of communication channel.

- **Interaction:** Information presented to your employees can be further filtered based on the specific interaction taking place. For example, if a customer calls to discuss an ongoing service issue, frontline staff should be able to quickly view the thread of all previous interactions relating to that issue—even if other personnel were involved. Similarly, a salesperson should be able to view the history, documents, and other information about a customer, without sorting through a great deal of unrelated data.

- **Multichannel:** Frontline staff should also have access to records of all customer communications, regardless of the channel used. If a customer first phones, then later emails, all related information should be available to anyone who may interact with that customer. By leveraging a common knowledge foundation across all communication channels, you can ensure that your organization is providing customers with consistent information, regardless of how you interact with customers.

Other factors can also help determine what information should be available to frontline staff. For example, certain government regulations may require protection of customer confidentiality, so certain personal information may have to be hidden from view. Or you may want to grant preferred partners access to information resources not available to other partners.

How should you provide knowledge?

Different modes of presentation are more suitable for different types of information, so you must determine how to best present various types information to frontline staff. Some suggestions follow.

- **Task-specific dynamic workspaces:** Using information about a customer, certain solutions tailor content and functionality on the agent's desktop to address the issue at hand. Certain fields and tabs can be dynamically displayed or hidden in the workspace based on the context of the interaction.

- **Alerts and notifications:** Bringing immediate attention to certain issues with on-screen, email, or voice and text messages is important. Managers can be notified when call wait-times exceed a specified threshold or when a deadline is approaching, and can take appropriate action. Notifying frontline employees that a particular event has occurred can also be helpful. A contact center agent who has been dealing with a customer's delayed order, when notified that the order has shipped, can let the customer know the expected delivery date.

- **Workflow prompts:** Using business rules, frontline staff can be prompted to ask certain questions or take certain actions. For example, customer service staff can be prompted to offer up-sell promotions to customers fitting a certain profile.

- **Integrated access to back-end systems:** Frontline contact center employees often need ready access to a wide range of systems such as order fulfillment, credit card authorization, or billing. Access to these systems should be incorporated into an agent desktop that eliminates multiple log-ins or toggling between desktop applications, which slows employees and delays responses to customers.

Designing desktop workspaces that accommodate all these requirements for a variety of frontline roles can be challenging. Be sure to choose technology that lets you easily modify screen elements and make changes as needs evolve.

Implementing knowledge-driven applications that facilitate delivery of relevant content to frontline users' desktops will help to improve the customer experiences these employees deliver. The more effectively you empower staff with knowledge, the more effectively they can respond to customer needs.

Once employees are prepared to address customer requests, the next step is to ensure that they can fully and consistently share knowledge with customers, regardless of communication channel—as detailed in the next chapter.

Doing It Right: Orbitz

Goals:
- Deliver a competitively differentiated customer experience.
- Stay current on ever-changing information about vendors, travel conditions, and industry regulations.
- Support multiple brands efficiently.
- Control contact center costs.

The Challenge: Deliver current knowledge to contact center agents

The online travel business is highly competitive and increasingly commoditized. Dozens of websites allow customers to book flights and hotels at discount prices. To successfully compete, market leader Orbitz needed to differentiate itself while controlling costs. The company also had to maintain the most current information about various vendors, changing travel conditions, and evolving industry regulations.

The Solution: An organized, segmented knowledge foundation

Orbitz created and diligently manages a large, well-organized knowledge foundation. It is continuously updated by subject-matter specialists who track the industry and make appropriate content changes immediately. This up-to-the-minute knowledge enables agents to effectively serve customers, typically resolving issues with a single call. And because agents are automatically informed of new information, they rarely require additional training.

Using the knowledge foundation, staff can also create an answer that addresses a certain issue and, with simple modifications, can make brand-specific versions for use by other Orbitz brands such as CheapTickets and Travelport—a process that saves the company time and money.

In addition, Orbitz has segmented the information in its knowledge foundation. Some content is available to the public via Web self-service; other information about business process and policies, site features and functions, and vendor relationships is available to contact center agents only.

Achievements:
- Top rankings have been repeatedly received for customer service and support.
- Self-service and first-call resolution rates are high.
- Agent error rates are low.
- A single solution supports multiple brands in delivering exceptional customer experiences.

Chapter 4
Offer Multichannel Choice

"It is the ability to choose which makes us human."
– Madeleine L'Engle

When interacting with organizations, today's customers expect to have a range of options—phone, email, website, chat, online forums and communities, fax, traditional mail, and in person. Because many customers will use them interchangeably, these options must be integrated to ensure a single, unified dialogue with each customer.

The challenges of multichannel communications
Following the "bouncing customer"
Customers will often jump from channel to channel in the course of a single incident. For example, a customer may email with a question and follow up with a phone call if he or she doesn't fully understand a reply or if the reply doesn't fully address an issue.

These calls can be especially frustrating for customers if phone agents don't have immediate access to information about customers' previous interactions with the organization. Customers can quickly become annoyed when they are asked to explain problems several times or when someone suggests a solution they've already tried. Such redundant conversations can alienate customers and reduce your staff's productivity.

To deliver consistently excellent customer experiences while offering customers a choice of communication channels, all customer interactions must be handled in a unified manner.

Everyone interacting with customers should be able to see all relevant previous exchanges with each customer, regardless of which channels were used. Information about previous exchanges should be current and complete, so that contact center agents can deal appropriately with customers. Agents will be best prepared to deal with customers' emotions, preferences, and special sensitivities if they can view notes from other agents about previous interactions as well as information from other departments, such as sales and marketing.

Unified channel management also eliminates redundancies that result from customers contacting you with the same request via multiple channels. Customers often call an organization if they haven't received a response to an email within a few hours. Unfortunately, in many contact centers, channels are separately managed. When customers both call and email a company about a single issue, their emails may be answered even after the very same issues have already been resolved by phone. In a contact center with unified channel management, agents are aware of all previous communications and can ask customers' permission to delete the redundant communication.

Providing consistent information
Receiving different information through different channels is confusing for customers. For example, if a call center agent provides information that is inconsistent with your website, your customers won't trust either source. Some customers may even try to take advantage of inconsistencies by contacting a company numerous times through different channels, attempting to get the answer they want—which may obligate your company to accept a merchandise return or provide a discount that is not consistent with official policies.

By leveraging a common knowledge foundation across all communication channels, you can ensure that your organization is providing customers with consistent information regardless of how you interact with customers. The content used by employees who interact with customers by phone, email, chat, or traditional mail should come from the same source as the content provided through online self-service options. Use of a common knowledge foundation can also help to ensure that information shared with customers has been approved by legal staff, compliance teams, and corporate communications departments, if required.

Furthermore, a common knowledge foundation can help to determine when more information is needed. For example, when Nikon's customers consistently asked questions about a certain product feature, the company realized it needed to provide more detailed information about the feature through all customer communication channels and also improve product manuals.

Using a common knowledge foundation across all channels also improves efficiency and speeds an organization's response to changing circumstances. All relevant information can be added, deleted, or revised in a single place, instead of administering and synchronizing multiple repositories.

Hearing the customer's voice
With multiple communications channels, gaining visibility into customers' problems and preferences can be challenging. Your contact center may be able to report on top issues handled by phone in a given week but may not be able to produce similar reports for email or the Web—not a problem, if the majority of your customers interact with your or-

ganization by phone. But as your customers begin to interact with you through a variety of channels, limited reporting capabilities will hinder your ability to monitor and, if needed, improve the customer experience.

In addition, channel-specific reports can be misleading. Customers may contact you by phone about issues that they perceive as significant, but may use your website to resolve problems they consider less important. In such a situation, overreliance on call center reports may draw your company's attention and resources toward a seemingly significant problem, which in fact is being experienced by only a small percentage of customers who contact you by phone. Meanwhile, a much greater percentage of customers may be experiencing another issue—one that truly requires your company's attention—but because they are attempting to resolve it via the Web, you may not be immediately aware of it.

Consolidating feedback reporting across all channels into a common system ensures that you will hear the customer's voice, regardless of how he or she chooses to interact with you.

Reducing and aligning communication costs
The cost of each customer interaction depends, in part, on the channel used. As mentioned earlier, a phone call handled by an agent is more expensive than one handled by voice self-service, and an email is more expensive than a Web self-service interaction.

Sending customers to the best and most cost-effective channel (known as "right-channeling") will benefit them as much as it does your organization. For example, if customers' routine, simple questions are answered via Web and voice self-service, contact center agents can devote more time to addressing issues that truly warrant personal attention and specific expertise.

Encouraging customers to use less-expensive channels can also result in significant cost savings. The companies profiled throughout this book have realized millions of dollars in cost reductions by shifting customer interactions from agent-assisted phone calls to Web and voice self-service systems.

Another reason for right-channeling customers is that you can optimize the return on every dollar spent on customer interactions by ensuring that the most appropriate channel is always used. For example, when a first-time customer purchases an inexpensive product and calls a company with questions, having a contact center agent handle the call is costly and may not be worth the expense. But having an agent speak with a repeat customer, who consistently purchases many high-priced items, is a worthwhile use of resources—and may even result in additional sales.

Optimizing the multichannel customer experience

As you seek to optimize your company's use of multiple channels, keep the following principles in mind.

Avoid the dead-end channel

If customers have trouble finding what they need through one channel, they should be able to quickly switch to a different channel. If they are unable to find what they need via self-service, they should be able to initiate email, chat, or phone contact. Without options, customers may become frustrated and may be disinclined to ever use self-service again.

Provide a channel for customers to connect with each other
Online communities, forums, or blogs can foster a sense of community and tap into the collective expertise of customers. These channels can also provide additional insight into what customers are thinking, because they may share opinions and information among themselves that they would not share directly with your organization.

For example, iRobot created an online discussion board so that customers could share their thoughts and experiences, which is particularly important when pioneering a new market such as vacuum robots. The discussion board is integrated with the company's contact center software, so anyone dealing with a customer can see his or her entire interaction history—including all phone calls, emails, and discussion board postings—in a single view, providing an up-to-the-minute status report on that customer.

Considering today's online environment, in all likelihood a customer community will develop around an organization's products or services whether the organization is involved or not. By launching or sponsoring a customer community, however, you can facilitate its growth, remain apprised of customers' interests and concerns, and potentially influence community discussions. You can also leverage the content of forums and blogs by incorporating it into your knowledge foundation. Both employees and customers can then access the information generated through these channels.

Extend traditional channels through conferences and events

Another way to build stronger relationships with customers and foster a greater sense of community is to stage events that bring them together. Such events can include regional meetings or events scheduled in conjunction with key industry trade shows. These events can include educational presentations, product demonstrations, and discussion groups that allow customers to share successes and challenges. They can also include activities that provide an opportunity for customers to socialize and network. A large, costly program isn't necessary. You can begin by renting a conference room at a local hotel and bringing a few customers together for a candid exchange of insights and ideas. Often, the customers who attend initial events understand their value—and will volunteer to help engage other customers. Many organizations that begin on a modest scale are able to expand these events into successful annual conferences attended by hundreds of customers and partners.

Avoid adding new channels until existing ones are functioning optimally

Be sure that current communication channels are meeting customers' expectations and needs before launching new ones. For example, enhance and streamline customers' phone interactions before adding a chat channel, or you may overload contact center agents. In such a case, implementing voice self-service before chat may be a better option, as it can help to streamline customers' phone interactions, minimize wait times, and reduce agent workloads.

Always measure the quality of the customer experience in its true, multichannel context

When measuring contact resolution rates, be sure to consider all interactions with a customer, through all channels, regarding a single issue. As noted previously, a customer may visit a website first for information but, not finding it, may email the company and then follow up with a phone call if he or she doesn't receive a prompt response. While the issue may be resolved during a single phone conversation, this example represents a third-contact resolution. Customers who have to contact a company three times before receiving the information they need are not likely to describe the interaction as positive.

Doing It Right: Nikon

Goals:
- Scale customer experience management capabilities to keep pace with a rapidly growing customer base.
- Support a premier brand with premier customer experience.
- Control costs.

The Challenge: Deliver a premier cross-channel customer experience

As the photography market's leading brand, Nikon is dedicated to delivering an excellent customer experience across all communication channels. Doing so is not easy for a company with a rapidly growing customer base and increasingly tight margins. When Nikon embarked on a customer experience initiative, growing sales were taxing existing resources and competitors were offering customers more product options.

The Solution: An integrated multichannel contact center system

Nikon's powerful contact center system integrates and optimizes customer communications via phone, email, and Web. The system enables contact center employees to view customers' complete service histories across all contact points—telephone, website, email, and fax—so they can efficiently provide personalized support.

The system allows incidents to be quickly routed or escalated across the company's various locations and tiers to the most appropriate individual. Built on a powerful knowledge foundation, the system ensures that both customers and Nikon staff can find approved, up-to-date, relevant answers to common questions, with just a few keystrokes.

This integrated, multichannel contact center system gives the company full visibility into its customers' issues and concerns, enabling the company to respond quickly when necessary. In addition, it provides valuable information to Nikon's designers and marketers, allowing them to quickly react to the changing needs of the buying public.

Achievements:
- Customer satisfaction scores consistently exceed 95 percent across all channels.
- A 50 percent reduction in call response times has been achieved.
- Email response times have reduced by 70 percent.
- The contact center headcount has been reduced despite the tripling of unit sales.

Chapter 5
Listen to Your Customers

"Know how to listen, and you will profit even from those who talk badly."

– Plutarch

Delivering a consistently excellent customer experience is impossible if you don't have a systematic way to determine what your customers are thinking. You must understand customers' opinions on everything from the quality of your products to the helpfulness of your website. By listening to and learning from customers, you will gain valuable feedback that can guide your entire organization in delivering outstanding customer experiences. In addition, you can intervene and correct problems immediately, before they escalate into a crisis situation.

Techniques for improving listening skills
Capture feedback at the "moment of truth"

Discovering that a customer is dissatisfied about an incident that occurred six months ago gives you little, if any, opportunity to correct the situation. At that point, the customer is probably hesitant to interact with your company again and may have already taken his or her business elsewhere. And yet many companies survey customers only once or twice a year. To preserve and strengthen relationships with customers, your organization should be aware of anything that may threaten a relationship—at the actual time of the interaction, the "moment of truth." To achieve this, ask customers for feedback during or immediately after interactions, and make it easy for them to respond. For example, automatically email customers a short survey after they have completed a customer service call or received a shipment. After a chat session ends, present the customer with questions on a Web page or use automated voice technology to solicit feedback via phone. Requesting customer feedback at the "moment of truth" typically drives greater response rates than do traditional, periodic surveys. Such outreach will provide continuously updated customer satisfaction metrics, organized by channel. Also, if employees are immediately alerted when customers are not satisfied, they can quickly intervene and correct problems.

In addition, certain software programs can be used to detect emotional content by analyzing the language used in customers' email; when dissatisfaction or frustration is identified, emails can be routed to appropriate individuals for accelerated attention.

Regardless of the method used, capture feedback at the precise moment an interaction occurs, and if necessary act immediately. Doing so will typically increase survey response rates from low, single-digit percentages to 35 or 40 percent.

When surveying customers, keep questions as brief as possible. For example, ask customers to rate your organization, using a numeric scale, on helpfulness, speed of response, and level of professionalism. Always ask for additional comments so customers can provide more detailed feedback. If you are using automated surveys, provide a way for customers to contact someone directly, in real time; with this option, you will be informed of urgent issues. Be cautious of inundating customers with feedback requests; by building business rules into a survey system, you can control how often an individual is surveyed.

Traditional broad-based, batch surveys, done periodically, do provide value. Product development teams can survey customers before designing new or improved products, and marketers can use feedback to develop special promotions or refine the tone and content of messaging. As your organization collects more detailed information about customers, you'll be able to target surveys based on multiple customer attributes. You'll also find that as use of multiple communication channels matures, you'll be able to execute surveys more effectively and cost-efficiently by leveraging email, the Web, chat and automated voice systems.

Accentuate the negative

While only a small percent of customers may provide negative feedback, this information is the most valuable because it will reveal what you must improve. Even a small number of customers can adversely influence many others, through online review sites, forums, blogs, or word of mouth. Keep in mind that the number of complaints registered may not adequately reflect the number of dissatisfied customers—many people won't take time to express their opinions. So when reviewing complaints, assume that they are just the visible tip of the iceberg. Most important, complaints highlight areas that are detracting from the customer experience and require attention. A company's willingness to uncover and remedy customer dissatisfaction can truly set it ahead of competitors. One note of caution: Don't let high or improved customer satisfaction scores allow you to become less diligent. Maintaining customer satisfaction is an ongoing effort.

Act on what you learn

When organizations learn of customer issues, they must act quickly to correct them—not weeks or months later. Rapid, appropriate responses to customer problems can actually strengthen relationships and increase loyalty. You need to capture customer feedback in real time, act on that feedback immediately, and demonstrate how that feedback has changed the way you do business. And if you aren't going to use feedback to improve the customer experience, don't bother asking for it.

The following steps will help to ensure that captured feedback is used to correct problems and improve performance:

- **Automatically route negative feedback** to the appropriate individual or department for fast action. Require that the person responsible contact the customer within a certain number of hours.

- **Implement workflow rules** that automatically notify managers of specific events, such as a customer who expresses dissatisfaction or gives an agent a low rating.

- **Send a weekly report** of all product-related complaints to product and manufacturing managers.

- **Analyze feedback,** and if needed, summarize or aggregate it, so others can understand implications, spot trends, and take appropriate action.

- **Periodically report** feedback trends to executive management.

In addition to sharing negative feedback with the appropriate individuals or teams within your organization, be sure to track issues and complaints through final resolution.

When trends emerge, such as a number of customers complaining about similar issues, quickly determine and correct the root cause. Staff may need more training, a product or policy may require modification, or the knowledge foundation may need to be updated. Taking remedial action to eliminate the cause prevents similar problems from occurring, which will enhance the overall customer experience while controlling support costs.

Make feedback accessible and useable

In addition to triggering corrective actions, customer feedback should be retained and made readily available to all employees involved with customer interactions. A typical approach is to include feedback in the common customer record. Captured feedback can then be used to provide personalized service. For example, if contact center agents know that certain customers tend to complain about lengthy shipping times, they can suggest expedited shipping.

Inform customers that you've acted on their input

When customers provide feedback, close the loop. Thank them and let them know whenever you act on it. When customers take time to provide input and receive no response, they are less likely to provide feedback in the future.

Ways to demonstrate to customers that their feedback is valued and has been acted upon include the following:

- **General notifications** inform all customers about changes made in response to their collective input, such as product modification or service policy changes.

- **Targeted notifications** inform groups of customers that the issues they've raised have been addressed. Such notifications typically relate to a certain product, service, or policy and don't apply to all customers.

- **Individual notifications** inform a single customer about an outcome driven by his or her feedback, such as changes to your return policy, based on the customer's response to a survey.

By encouraging customers to respond to these notifications, you may be able to foster ongoing dialog with insightful or supportive customers. Customer responses will help you determine the effectiveness of your notifications.

Emphasize the importance of the customer's voice
The strength of a company's brand and its business performance depends to a great degree on how well it understands and responds to customers. To build a truly customer-focused culture, employees must know that customer feedback is highly valued and that it influences an organization's strategy and tactics.

One way to instill the importance of the customer voice in your frontline staff is to regularly share and discuss customer satisfaction ratings, which indicate whether you're listening to and responding to customers. Tying compensation to customer satisfaction—such as giving financial rewards to individuals, teams, or the entire company when satisfaction scores improve—can be highly motivating. An alternative to financial rewards is finding a way to recognize and celebrate contributions of groups or individuals who have enhanced the customer experience. Let employees know when you make changes based on customer feedback, and show them the tangible business benefits of those changes, such as faster production times or significant cost savings.

For example, TomTom, a leading manufacturer of personal navigation devices, considers customer feedback so essential to its ongoing success that all customer-facing staff, including the company's board of directors, are required to spend two hours each month listening in to customer calls.

Improvements in customer satisfaction rankings can also be used to demonstrate the value of new processes or technology to upper management and can potentially justify additional investment. In addition, positive customer satisfaction rankings can be used in public relations, advertising, and branding, while providing additional recognition and motivation to employees who interact with customers.

Doing It Right: Black & Decker

Goals:

- Make the entire company more responsive to customers.
- Optimize performance and efficiency of customer service across all channels.
- Use customer feedback to make better business decisions.

The Challenge: Create an efficient, customer-centric organization

Black & Decker wanted to leverage customers' phone, email, and Web interactions with its contact centers in order to capture valuable, timely information that company managers could use to make better-informed decisions. The global market leader would use feedback to design better products, improve manufacturing quality, market more efficiently, and sell more effectively.

The Solution: Centralized management of customer interactions

Customer feedback across all channels is captured in a central repository and automatically distributed to employees. Business rules ensure that incidents associated with specific products are forwarded to the appropriate product manager. The real-time feedback gives product managers a sense of how their products are faring in the marketplace—especially important with new product releases.

With a single repository and easy access to all data about customer questions, complaints, and feedback, agents are able to address customer issues quickly and effectively. Real-time alerts sent to the company's manufacturing teams enable agents to detect patterns in customer complaints and take corrective action immediately. For example, Black & Decker received feedback that helped identify a small, inexpensive part that hadn't been machined correctly. Engineering and manufacturing teams were able to make a quick change, preventing many customers from experiencing problems while saving the company thousands of dollars in potential returns.

Similar information is made available to the marketing and sales departments via periodic reports, and customized business rules alert the legal department when a product liability issue emerges during a customer call.

Achievements:
- Rich, actionable customer insights are delivered to product management, manufacturing, and other departments.
- Real-time alerts prevent costly, large-scale product returns.

Chapter 6
Design Seamless Experiences

"We must all hang together now, or assuredly we shall hang separately."
— Benjamin Franklin

If you've ever phoned a company to ask about a special offer you received in the mail and found that the agent knew nothing about the offer, or if you've received a sales call from a company when you can't get its service department to return your calls, you've experienced the negative effects of a "siloed" organization. In many organizations, multiple teams interact with customers, yet they don't work closely with one another or communicate frequently; sometimes, they even use different systems and processes. The result is a less-than-optimal customer experience.

Today's customers expect everyone they interact with at an organization—regardless of function or department—to have access to current information about them and all their previous interactions with the company. When boundaries exist between departments, groups, or individuals, and customer information is not shared, the quality of the customer experience is undermined.

Tear down the silos
To break down operational walls, consider your organization from the customer's perspective. Do business with your own company, and evaluate your own experience. Think about how customers will interact with the organization during the course of a transaction or process. Who will customers deal with at each stage? What do customers expect from company representatives? What information will the customer be asked

to provide? Will he or she be requested to provide it several times? Addressing these questions is a first step in overcoming operational boundaries and beginning to design a more seamless and satisfying customer experience.

Consider the following example of how a retail store opening may be experienced from a customer's perspective. The diagram illustrates how a single customer experience can encompass interactions with multiple, separate parts of a business—and how those parts must share information and work together to ensure a seamless customer experience.

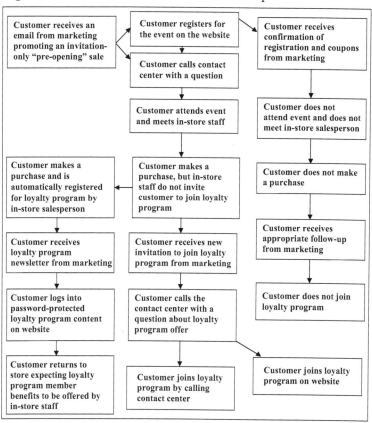

This example demonstrates how each step in a business process that engages customers is part of the overall experience—and how each should be designed from the customer's perspective. Each interaction should also provide some type of value to customers in terms of enhancing their experience with your company.

Designing elements for the customer experience

As you design cross-departmental processes and workflows that affect the customer experience, consider how these can be automated with appropriate software applications. Automating multistep customer interactions that involve independently operating teams will ensure that customer experiences will be seamless—even though multiple handoffs between departments and teams may occur. Be sure that anyone interacting with customers can easily escalate issues—for instance, encourage contact center staff to alert field support of significant problems.

The following list of guidelines will help you effectively automate customer experience workflows across your organization.

- **Track customer knowledge via attributes:** During any given interaction, your frontline staff may need to review or modify attributes in the customer record, such as identifying which products a customer uses, noting a change of address, or adding details gleaned through conversation that can be used to personalize future interactions.

  Customer attributes should be current, accurate, and easily accessible by anyone who works with customers.

This information can be used to provide specialized attention, such as discounts based on past purchases. Your ability to execute such actions—which can often generate additional business—will be largely contingent upon the quality of your customer data.

For example, Shaklee Corporation uses customer data to deliver tailored messages to specific target audiences and track which customers respond to each communication. Customers receive only relevant information, and the company's targeted outreach has greatly improved campaign response rates.

- **Assign tasks to employees' desktops:** One of the most basic requirements for enabling a well-designed customer experience is the ability to automatically prompt employees anywhere in the organization (and sometimes outside the organization, if you're using outsourcers or partners) to perform certain tasks, such as calling a customer, approving an exception to company policy, or reviewing performance metrics.

Typically, a control mechanism, such as an event trigger, is associated with each task. For example, a reminder can be sent to employees who haven't performed a task within a specified amount of time, or a supervisor can be alerted when a deadline is missed.

- **Define and modify workflow rules:** Authorized managers must be able to define, implement, and modify various workflow rules such as yes/no decision trees and event triggers. These rules will help managers be aware of and able to respond quickly to many situations, from individual customer requests to sudden spikes in call wait times.

Giving managers the ability to implement and change workflow rules without the help of technical staff is essential, because business conditions and requirements change quickly. During peak seasonal periods, for example, it may be necessary to change the routing of incoming calls. By empowering nontechnical staff to make these adjustments, you can accelerate your responsiveness to customers while avoiding the bottlenecks that typically occur within busy IT departments. Ongoing refinement of workflow rules will improve both operational efficiencies and the customer experience.

- **Present content online:** Automating the customer experience requires the ability to present the right Web page to the right customer at the right time. For example, frequent buyers or members of a customer loyalty program who click on a "help" link in the midst of an online purchase can be offered chat support.

Giving nontechnical staff tools that allow them to post and unpost Web content without the assistance of IT, such as technical alerts or time-sensitive promotions, is also important. Your organization must be able to change online content quickly in response to changing market dynamics, actions of competitors, or other conditions.

- **Automate certain customer communications:** In many situations, automating communication with customers is the most efficient way to keep them informed of relevant news. During peak buying seasons, for example, customers may appreciate being notified of free shipping offers. You can notify customers that service contracts should be renewed, that account payments are overdue, or that new product models are available.

Outbound communications with customers are an essential part of any well-managed customer experience. This important proactive step is covered in more detail in the next chapter.

Doing It Right: Shaklee

Goals:

- Reinforce relationship-based business model with a superior member experience.
- Support brand promise with consistent, high-quality member interactions.
- Turn around stagnant sales and regain market leadership.

The Challenge: Boosting sales and regaining market leadership

Shaklee grew to be the largest natural nutrition company in the United States by building a quality brand and growing its direct sales model. But increasing competition and the advent of the Web challenged the company's brand dominance and its ability to sustain the relationships that made it a market leader. In order to boost sales, revitalize the Shaklee brand, and regain market leadership, Shaklee needed to provide a superior customer experience during all customer interactions, regardless of touch point or department.

The Solution: Link marketing, sales, and service

Shaklee instituted common processes across sales, marketing, and customer service so that customers receive the same quality of service across all interactions. All departments also have access to the common knowledge foundation, enabling all employees to respond consistently to customer questions. In addition, the knowledge foundation provides employees with visibility into a customer's complete history with Shaklee, eliminating the need for customers to repeat information as they transition across departments or interaction channels.

Shaklee also uses insights gleaned through its service interactions to better target outbound communications. Before contacting a customer, salespeople can check whether a customer has unresolved service issues; in this way, they avoid being blindsided when trying to make a sale. Shaklee takes cross-department collaboration one step further by feeding customer insight back into product development, which influences product design and enables cross-function product launches.

How do customers benefit from this integrated approach? They receive personalized treatment regardless of which department they interact with or how they interact with it. Shaklee benefits, too—from increased productivity and efficiency across marketing, sales, and service operations.

Achievements:
- Providing a consistently exceptional experience across all communication channels that customers use.
- Maintaining a customer satisfaction score of 89 percent, with a double-digit growth in sales.

Chapter 7
Engage Proactively with Customers

"What we've got here is a failure to communicate."
– From Cool Hand Luke

To deliver an outstanding experience, you must proactively interact with customers. Answering potential questions before they ask, providing them with information before they need it, and personalizing communications based on previous interactions are all examples of proactive, exceptional customer service.

Yet many companies take the "emergency room" approach to dealing with customers. They wait until the "patient" is brought in on a stretcher in a crisis situation, and then everyone rushes to remedy the situation. Little consideration is given to what caused the problem; the focus is on fixing it and sending the patient on his or her way. As any health professional will tell you, however, real success comes when you can keep patients out of the emergency room altogether. That's why your doctor tells you to eat right, get plenty of exercise, and go for regular checkups that can catch potential problems before they adversely impact your health.

In much the same way, you should prescribe changes within your organization to eliminate factors that erode customer satisfaction. By understanding your customers and their history with your company, and by interacting with them accordingly, you can move your customer experience from the emergency room to the fitness center. Once you begin to anticipate customers' needs and preempt problems, their satisfaction levels will rise, loyalty will increase, and you'll see fewer customers defecting.

A robust knowledge foundation and its effective use are key to successful, proactive customer interactions. By using customer knowledge correctly, you can proactively interact with customers in an intelligent, compelling manner. In the process, you can develop long-term loyal relationships and customer advocates.

For example, while sending out generic messages to customers can sometimes generate response rates of 1 to 3 percent, most customers will view them as unwanted and irrelevant. After receiving inappropriate communications, customers sense that a company doesn't know who they are and cares little about them as individuals. In addition, customers are less likely to pay attention to subsequent communications sent their way—even if those messages are relevant. Beyond eroding customer relationships, untargeted customer communications drive up costs—with limited return.

Key principles of effective customer communications

When communicating proactively with customers, keep the following principles in mind:

- **Segmentation:** Information should be delivered only to customers for whom it is relevant. Relevance should be based on customer attributes, such as the customer's location or past purchase history. If your communications aren't appropriately segmented, customers may deny you the right to communicate with them further. With email, for example, consistent relevance is particularly important because customers who receive several irrelevant messages may not open your emails and may even opt out of future mailings. Also, you may want to exclude customers with open support incidents from certain distribution lists. A combination of a knowledge foundation and the appropriate analytical tools can provide a great deal of customer insight to be used for segmentation purposes. Once you've segmented customers, determine how to proactively engage with each segment in the most appropriate manner; some may appreciate and respond to marketing offers and up-sell/cross-sell promotions, while other may be interested in receiving payment reminders and alerts about expiring warranties and contracts.

- **Personalization:** Customer communications should be as personalized as possible. Always include the recipient's name rather than a generic greeting. To deliver communications that solicit favorable responses, send messages that address customers' individual needs and desires—messages that relate to the reasons a customer does business with you. Communications should reflect knowledge of specific interactions with each customer. For example, if a new accessory is available for a certain product, notify only those customers who have purchased that product. Your customer knowledge foundation will help identify what types of communications will be most relevant to each segment.

- **Authenticity:** Consumers, barraged by a constant onslaught of companies vying for their business, welcome authentic communications delivered by people who seem to know and care about them. Because authenticity is easier to detect in voice, tone, and manner, call centers are often an ideal place to begin incorporating behaviors that will appeal to customers. If frontline staff members convey knowledge during each interaction and consistently demonstrate that they're passionate about helping customers solve problems, customers are more likely to trust that your company will deliver on its promises.

- **Timing and frequency:** Be sure that you don't overcommunicate with customers. Unless customers have specifically requested more, I recommend no more than two communications each month. Also, make sure that your communications are properly timed—allow a minimum of a week between each.

Using a campaign management solution that leverages a robust customer knowledge foundation and offers intelligent, multichannel, event-triggered campaigns can be one of the most effective ways to engage with customers proactively. The value of such tools is their ability to push information and content out to customers through the right channel at the right time.

Right Start, a specialty retailer of juvenile products, learned that, to succeed as a multichannel retailer, its online channel needed to support its brick-and-mortar business—rather than compete with it. By leveraging data from the company's website, Right Start is able to execute campaigns for specific locations, which has helped build stronger relationships with local customers and increase store traffic.

Implementing proactive communications
The principles of segmentation, personalization, authenticity, and timing and frequency can be applied in various ways to proactively engage with customers and enhance the customer experience. A number of examples follow.

Demographic targeting

This classic marketing strategy entails tailoring communications to customers with specific attributes such as gender, geographic location, or income level. For example, middle-aged men would receive information about certain products and promotions, much different from that sent to young mothers.

Calendar-driven promotions

Seasonal promotions can be an effective way to reach out to customers. During spring months, travel companies can alert customers of upcoming summer vacation specials. In late fall, online retailers can remind customers of free shipping on holiday items. Companies that capture personal data such as customers' birthdays or anniversaries sometimes extend special offers as those dates approach.

Event-based communications

Specific events can create unique opportunities to inform and engage customers. An airline may need to alert specific travelers when bad weather threatens to disrupt travel plans. Shortly after customers purchase certain items, companies can inform them of related accessories or service contracts. Less-than-positive experiences, such as late deliveries or malfunctioning products, can also trigger outreach, such as an apology or a discount coupon. Individual customer events, such as marriage or change of address, can also be used to generate personalized communications.

Behavior-based communications

Close observation of customer behaviors may also lead you to reach out to customers with specific messages or promotions. For example, if a frequent customer stops making purchases for a period of time, contact him or her to inquire about potential problems. If a customer's buying volume suddenly jumps, let him or her know about special services for preferred customers. By tracking and analyzing customer behavior, you may detect patterns—such as spikes in purchases at certain times of the year—and respond with a timely offer or incentive.

These behavior-based communications can involve a combination of segmentation and personalization. For example, a demographically segmented promotional mailing may also include a personalized greeting and acknowledgement of a recent purchase. An event-driven promotion can be enhanced with offers tailored for specific demographic segments.

To execute successful proactive communications, you must first lay the groundwork that will enable your organization to deliver a differentiated customer experience, as described in previous chapters. With a strong knowledge foundation, you will have information that will help in targeting customers appropriately. Using the knowledge foundation, frontline staff will be informed and able to respond to customers in a timely manner. And by implementing automated workflow processes, you can ensure that your communications are timely, relevant, and cost effective.

Following are several additional capabilities needed to communicate effectively with your customers.

Flexible list management and segmentation
To effectively segment customers and send tailored communications, you must be able to easily search and sort your customer database according to any attribute or set of attributes.

With this capability, you can ensure that only relevant, appropriate communications are sent to each customer.

Compelling content development

To engage customers in ongoing dialogue, you need to use state-of-the-art tools to create appealing communications, such as email invitations, that result in high response rates. To maximize effectiveness, these messages should include links to additional, relevant information that may be of interest to recipients, as well as a persuasive "call to action"—such as an offer to participate in a customer forum or a request to complete a survey—that entices customers to further engage with you.

Opt-in/opt-out controls

To respect customer preferences and comply with regulatory mandates, you must to be able to scrupulously enforce opt-in and opt-out requests. For example, the U.S. CAN-SPAM (Controlling the Assault of Non-Solicited Pornography and Marketing) Act requires commercial emailers to provide an opt-out link in every message. To ensure compliance, you need a mechanism that automatically makes the appropriate change in your customer database whenever a customer clicks the opt-out link.

Regardless of how you communicate with customers, always give them the ability to opt out of any type of communication. Centrally managing all outbound communication channels will prevent duplicative effort and ensure that customers are contacted through their preferred channels.

Collaborative content review

Before sending any communications to customers, have them reviewed by others within your organization, across a number of departments, such as marketing, product management, and legal. Automated workflow and collaborative tools can streamline and accelerate the review process.

Message testing and analysis

When doing large-scale mailings, send out test messages to sample groups to determine effectiveness. With content development tools, you can experiment with different message parameters, such as wording, layout, color, and graphics; analytic tools can be used to measure the impact these have on response rates.

Delivery management

To ensure that your online communications reach the intended recipients, you should comply with industry email standards and regulations, and work with large domains (such as AOL and Yahoo!) to avoid having your messages blocked or added to blacklists. Many companies and consultants specialize in email marketing strategies and execution, and can provide expertise.

Customized business rules

Applying a variety of business rules to proactive messaging can also enhance the effectiveness of customer communications. For example, implement a policy that prevents any customer from receiving more than two email messages each month—even if analysis using certain parameters indicates that a number of planned proactive communications are relevant to the customer.

You can also apply business rules to automated voice technology for another cost-effective way to proactively communicate with customers. For example, you can notify certain customers of upcoming events, past due balances, or expiring service contracts.

If you are diligent about ensuring that communications to customers always contain relevant, useful information, then your customers are much more likely to open, read, and potentially act after receiving them, rather than opt out. Once you've mastered how to proactively engage with customers, the next step is to further refine and enhance your customer experience using a process of continuous measurement and improvement.

Doing It Right: Right Start

Goals:
- Ensure that communications to every recipient are relevant.
- Grow both online and brick-and-mortar channels.
- Streamline and automate campaign design, execution, and management.

The Challenge: Support multiple channels and changing customer needs

Right Start has become the nation's leading specialty retailer of juvenile products by successfully leveraging its brick-and-mortar stores, e-commerce site, and direct mail catalog. Supporting these multiple retail channels can be challenging, because customers' needs change quickly as children grow.

The Solution: Deliver the right message at the right time

Right Start is successfully meeting these challenges with intelligent database management and point-and-click email campaign execution. The company tracks the age and gender of customers' children along with their product preferences. By doing so, the company can offer products for newborns to new mothers and later offer the same customers products for toddlers.

Right Start supports its brick-and-mortar channel by sending local customers notifications and coupons for a local store sale. It also alerts customers to store openings in other locations, in case they have friends or relatives living near the new store. By giving existing customers a coupon for a local store and another to pass along to someone near a new store, Right Start reinforces the loyalty of existing customers and frequently wins new ones.

Achievements:

- Targeted, personalized communications have led to 100 percent growth of the online channel.
- At the same time, the brick-and-mortar channel has seen 20 percent growth.

Chapter 8
Measure and Improve Continuously

"Measure what is measurable, and make measurable what is not so."
— Galileo Galilei

The seven steps previously described are the foundation for providing a great customer experience. Thousands of organizations have been able to significantly—and quickly—improve the customer experience by implementing these best practices. But providing an exceptional customer experience is a process, not a single event. Because market conditions, competitors, and consumer expectations are always changing, you must continuously measure your performance and improve your processes to keep pace. At the same time, you must foster a culture that drives continuous improvement.

Continuous improvement
Ongoing fine-tuning of your customer experience is essential, because your customers will continue to interact with other companies. When customers have an outstanding experience with a company (whether it is your competitor or a company in a different market), their expectations rise. Their best customer experience (or an exceptional one they've heard about) becomes a benchmark. Because you'll be constantly compared to other companies, take note of those that are recognized for best-in-class service. In terms of customer experience, they are your true competitors.

Learn from the best and the worst
Many organizations and media outlets periodically recognize organizations for great customer service. Study the strategies

and tactics these winners use. Many of these can be replicated within your own organization. Also, interact with companies known for exceptional customer experiences, such as the organizations profiled in this book. Your experiences are likely to trigger ideas about how you can adapt their practices within your organization.

Conversely, real-life examples of horrible customer experiences are increasingly publicized within the media, online forums, social networking sites, and blogs. Use these case studies as a "what not to do" primer for yourself and your employees.

Monitor competitors

Always watch what other companies in your industry are doing. The best way to do this is to become a customer and experience how they interact with customers; you'll gain valuable insight about both their and your organization's customer experience.

Network with peers

Connect with other professionals who are focused on the customer experience. Many technology vendors provide opportunities through local user groups, seminars, and conferences. At a minimum, you should schedule and budget for yourself and others on your leadership team to annually attend a conference focused on the customer experience. These events can provide an optimal setting for exchange of ideas and input from others. Another way to keep current with customer experience standards is to become affiliated with professional organizations focused on customer service. These groups also sponsor events for learning and networking, publish journals, and host blogs and forums. Or take the initiative yourself—form your own peer group with noncompetitors. Learning about their successes and understanding the pitfalls they have overcome will be helpful as you continue to improve your own customer experience.

Become your own customer

Engage with your own organization as a customer or have a friend or relative do so. Your company's policies and practices may look entirely different when you experience them from the customer's perspective.

Use mystery shoppers

You can contract with a company to measure the quality of your service through mystery shoppers, who interact with your organization as typical consumers and report on the experience. Mystery shoppers can be given questions to ask, complaints to make, specific items to buy, and measures to record, such as responses given to questions or time it takes to receive attention from an employee.

Take advantage of tune-ups

Your technology provider should offer free best-practice consultations at least twice annually. During these tune-ups, the vendor should review the quality of your customer experience and make recommendations for improvement.

Hire the pros

A professional services organization with customer experience expertise can be brought in to augment in-house resources or to do a limited-scope discovery engagement. A discovery engagement should include observing contact center agents at work, reviewing your website, and interviewing internal stakeholders. The results should include a list of recommended, prioritized customer experience projects as well as a comparison of your organization's customer experience with industry best practices. Such partners can accelerate time-to-benefit, but be sure to take an incremental approach to change.

Develop a road map for incremental improvements
When considering next steps, think modular, not monolithic. Incremental steps are the fastest path to improvement. Try implementing one improvement each quarter.

Periodically reapply the first seven steps
These steps can and should be repeatedly applied. Once completed, repeat them. You'll discover incremental areas of improvement that weren't obvious the first time, and but which will deliver significant value to your organization.

Measuring Performance
As you strive for continuous improvement, also monitor and measure your progress. With the customer experience scorecard (page 23), you can establish a baseline and determine which aspects of your customer experience need the most attention. As you implement improvements, continue to use the scorecard to assess ongoing progress, adding new assessment criteria as appropriate. After establishing a baseline, select metrics that are closely aligned with your organization's strategies and business goals. Most organizations err on the side of tracking too many metrics, when just a select few can be true indicators of the quality of the customer experience—in short, measure only what counts.

Traditional customer or contact center performance metrics, such as first contact resolution rate (FCRR), average call time, or transfer rates, are partial indicators of customer experience, but you also need to use metrics that track customer perceptions and satisfaction.

For example, TomTom tracks two key metrics related to its customer experience: how customers rate the company's customer service and whether customers would recommend TomTom to others.

Combined with traditional metrics, any of the following can be used to help gauge the quality of your customer experience. Be sure to compare performance to emerging trends and best practices.

- **Customer perceptions** of how well each interaction is handled can be assessed by several of the techniques for feedback capture, such as automated email, phone, or chat surveys (described in Chapter 5). In addition, phone, email, and chat conversations should be monitored to ensure that the words, phrases, and tone that employees use meet organizational standards.

- **Customer expectations** change over time. Periodic surveys will help in monitoring what customers want and expect.

- **Customer retention** can be derived by comparing the number of existing customers who make repeat purchases with the number of existing customers who should make repeat purchases. Other metrics to consider when analyzing customer retention rates are average transaction value, transaction frequency, and time between transactions, as appropriate for your company. For example, a clothing retailer may be interested in average transaction value and frequency of transactions, while a tire manufacturer may be more interested in the time between purchases.

- **Up-sell/cross-sell rates** gauge the success of generating revenue beyond an original order or reason for customer interaction. Many companies use up- and cross-sell rates as a performance measure in multichannel contact centers. Note that a focus on improving up-sell or cross-sell rates may increase the duration of customer interactions, which you should consider if using this metric in combination with service level measurements.

- **Conversion rate** refers to the percentage of customer interactions in which a sales opportunity occurs that translates into a sale. This can be measured as an absolute number of sales or as a percentage of interactions that result in a sale. As with up- and cross-sell rates, a focus on this metric may lengthen individual customer interactions.

One note of caution on using traditional contact center performance metrics: They can be misleading. For example, tracking and comparing the FCRRs for calls, email transactions, and Web interactions does provide insight into the quality of interactions conducted through each channel. But by the time customers call or email a company, they've probably already visited a website, bounced around a phone system, spoken with a store employee, or been confused by instructions in a product manual. As a result, what many companies view as FCRR actually represents second contact resolution rate (SCRR). To optimize true FCRR, you must ensure that customers receive the information they need during their first interaction with your company, regardless of how they choose to contact you.

In fact, the ultimate goal of any customer experience initiative should be a high zero contact resolution rate (ZCRR). Ideally, you should understand your customers well enough to anticipate their needs and address potential issues **before** they contact you. Many of the proactive communication strategies outlined in the previous chapter will help to improve FCRR and bring you closer to ZCRR.

Also, in measuring response rates for email and chat, remember that quality is more important than speed. Quick, shoddy responses will do more damage to customer relationships than will slightly delayed communications that completely address or resolve customer requests and issues.

Guidelines for using customer experience metrics

In addition to measuring and monitoring your organization's performance, use the metrics to drive actions and behaviors that continuously improve the customer experience. The following best practices will help you get the most value out of your customer experience metrics.

Communicate your goals

Everyone involved in your customer experience initiative should know which metrics have been defined as your key performance indicators (KPIs) and why. For example, if you establish your self-service usage goal to be 90 percent because other companies in your market have achieved this goal, communicate that to your team.

Make your goals visible

When motivating employees to work toward goals, making metrics readily available can help. Desktop dashboards will make it easy for staff to monitor performance and track progress. You can also post signage throughout the company location, promoting increases in your most important customer experience metrics.

Reward achievement

Positive reinforcement can help to foster customer-centric behaviors. Many of the methods described in Chapter 5, such as communicating goals, recognizing achievements, and celebrating progress, will help in fostering customer-centric behaviors. Competitions within teams or among groups can also help to boost performance. Many companies that focus on the customer experience tie employee compensation to customer satisfaction ratings or customer experience metrics.

Keep adjusting your goals

Be sure to periodically review and adjust your goals, because customer expectations will change over time, as will the capabilities of your company and competitors. Armed with metrics—and processes that use those metrics in effective, constructive ways—you will be able to continuously improve your customer experience.

Doing It Right: eHarmony

Goals:
- Deliver world-class customer care and personalized service.
- Answer customers' questions via the most appropriate channel.
- Closely monitor the "customer's voice."
- Control contact center costs.

The Challenge: Satisfy and retain fourteen million customers

Because eHarmony customers trust the company to help them find strong, satisfying relationships, they often require personalized assistance as they search and select potential matches. At the same time, eHarmony needs to control contact center costs to achieve profitability targets.

The Solution: Continuously improve the customer experience

By continuously evaluating and enhancing its self-service channel, eHarmony has been able to boost customer satisfaction. For example, the company built a knowledge foundation of 400 answers to typical questions, which customers can search by keyword, topic, or natural language query. Within a few months, this easy-to-use resource reduced email volume by 30 percent and brought email turnaround times down to a mere four hours for members.

As customers began to spend more time exploring the knowledge foundation, eHarmony added screen shots and other graphics to make the site easier to use, especially for online newcomers. Customers found this content so compelling, they began returning to the site more often. Call center agents, freed from answering many routine questions, can now spend much more time on the phone, coaching customers. As a result, customer satisfaction scores have soared. In addition, retention of customers who take advantage of eHarmony's trial subscription offer has tripled, allowing the company to grow by millions of customers annually.

Achievements:
- A 92 percent satisfaction rating has been achieved for phone service.
- The satisfaction rating for email support has passed 40 percent.
- The trial subscription retention rate has tripled.

Section III
Making It Happen

"I don't look to jump over seven-foot bars; I look around for one-foot bars that I can step over."
– Warren Buffet

Transforming a company's customer experience from adequate to outstanding requires deliberate, consistent action by many individuals throughout the company. It also requires leadership—someone must have the vision to champion change and the leadership skills to guide the organization to success.

If you are leading or involved in a customer experience initiative, keep the following guidelines in mind.

Take it step-by-step
Because optimization of the customer experience can require extensive change across many aspects of an organization, it can be tempting to launch a large project with lofty goals. Resist that temptation. Massive "boil-the-ocean" projects can overwhelm employees and drain budgets. Also, the greater the scope of your initiative, the more likely you are to encounter multiple pockets of resistance within the organization.

A more effective approach is to focus on a specific area until you achieve the desired results. Using an incremental approach, you can produce near-term results that will help to build credibility and gain support for your efforts; you may be able to achieve cost savings that can fund future stages of the project. Regardless of where you begin, keep overall goals in mind and consider your first step not in isolation but in the context of your final goals.

Do the right things in the right order

The eight steps described in Section II are listed in an order that has helped thousands of companies improve their customer experience. If you're not able to provide fast, accurate answers to customers' basic questions, trying to up-sell to them doesn't make sense. Likewise, adding a chat channel to your website when you're not providing good service through existing phone and email channels won't improve your customer experience.

Most organizations implement the eight steps in the order described here, but you may need to apply them in a slightly different order because of your specific situation.

Acquire technology wisely

Select a technology partner with a comprehensive offering that can be implemented in phases. Avoid both monolithic and point solutions. Consider the software-as-a-service (SaaS) model, also referred to as "on-demand software." With SaaS, applications are hosted and managed at a vendor's facility and delivered to user desktops via the Web. This approach enables you to avoid the capital costs and ongoing ownership burdens associated with conventionally deployed enterprise software. It lets you purchase specific pieces or modules of software functionality on an as-needed basis—rather than forcing you to make a significant up-front investment. And it allows you to remain focused on your business, not on managing your technology.

The SaaS model also simplifies the process of building a working pilot, quickly and at a reasonable cost. SaaS vendors, confident in their ability to deliver results, will typically help you launch a pilot even if you are not yet ready to make a major investment. Using the pilot to demonstrate the quantifiable impact the system can have on your business should help in gaining approval for additional investment.

Using the SaaS model, within 90 days most organizations can build a basic knowledge foundation, leverage the knowledge foundation to provide improved self-service options, and empower frontline employees. After accomplishing these first three steps, measure the results using the customer experience scorecard, and plan further refinements. Your customers will soon notice that doing business with your company is becoming easier and more convenient.

About Greg Gianforte

Greg Gianforte, CEO and founder of RightNow, has led the company from its founding in 1997 through ten consecutive years of revenue growth and a successful IPO. His market vision, leadership, entrepreneurial philosophy, and commitment to ethical business practices have enabled RightNow to consistently grow and to achieve remarkable levels of customer loyalty and satisfaction.

Greg is also the author of *Bootstrapping Your Business: Start and Grow a Successful Company with Almost No Money.*

Greg holds a BE in electrical engineering and an MS in computer science from Stevens Institute of Technology.

RightNow is headquartered in Bozeman, Montana, with additional offices in North America and in Europe and Asia.

For more information about how RightNow can help your company achieve its near- and long-term customer experience goals, please visit www.rightnow.com.

RightNow is a registered trademark of RightNow Technologies, Inc.